ISBN 1-58023-060-1

# The Way of Fla

## A GUIDE TO THE FORGOTTEN MYSTICAL TRADITION OF JEWISH MEDITATION

"There is a story: Once there was a fish who started wondering, where was the ocean? She had heard all her life about the ocean and how we are born and die in it—how it surrounds us and how, when we surrender to it, we gain enlightenment. All this sounded very exciting to her, and she was determined to find it. So she swam from sea to sea, asking everyone she met whether they knew where to find the ocean. As far as I know, she is swimming still."

*Open your soul to the sweetness of Jewish mysticism. Discover and explore the mystical path of Jewish meditation.*

With passion and humor, this powerful general guide incorporates philosophy and story with ideas for daily living—including suggestions for setting up your own meditative practice. Emphasizing the need for joy and community in meditation, Davis invites you to wander this extraordinary and compelling path of the heart—*hitlahavut,* the way of flame.

Davis combines traditional teachings and his own unorthodox experience, including a stint as a mendicant monk ("though in a Jewish sort of way") at a Catholic abbey in southern California, to offer a fresh and reinvigorated understanding of the spirit of Jewish meditation.

# THE WAY OF FLAME

## A Guide to the Forgotten Mystical Tradition of Jewish Meditation

by Avram Davis

For People of All Faiths, All Backgrounds
**Jewish Lights Publishing**

*The Way of Flame*
*A Guide to the Forgotten Mystical Tradition of*
*Jewish Meditation*

Copyright © 1996 by Avram Davis

**Library of Congress Cataloging-in-Publication Data**
Davis, Avram.
The way of flame : a guide to the forgotten mystical
tradition of Jewish meditation / by Avram Davis.
p.      cm.
Originally published: 1st ed. [San Francisco] :
HarperSanFrancisco, c1996.
ISBN 1-58023-060-1 (pbk.)
1. Meditation—Judaism. 2. Mysticism—Judaism.
3. Contemplation. 4. Spiritual life—Judaism. I. Title.
[BM723.D385      1999]
296.7'2—dc21                          99–36860
                                               CIP


ISBN 978-1-68336-450-4 (pbk)
ISBN 978-1-68336-451-1 (hc)

Manufactured in the United States of America

Cover design by Bridgett Taylor
Text design by Ralph Fowler
Set in Fairfield Light

*For People of All Faiths, All Backgrounds*
Published by Jewish Lights Publishing
www.jewishlights.com

# CONTENTS

*The root of everything*

*is meditation. It is a*

*very great and lofty*

*concept, making a*

*person worthy of all*

*holiness.... When a*

*person meditates he is*

*... attached to the*

*Infinite even with*

*regard to his mundane*

*bodily needs.*

Rebbe Chaim Azului,

*The Chida,* (1724–1806)

# INTRODUCTION

*Devekut [rapturous
attachment] is seventy
times more valuable
for the soul than
Torah study.*

Sefer Haredim

When I was twenty-three (many years ago), I went to Europe and then traveled overland to India. It was a sad and bitter time for me. My father and grandfather, both of whom I had been very close to, had died within months of each other. My grandfather died quickly and without pain, but my father had a hard dying. He struggled like a fish gutted by a hook and beating against the bottom of a boat, desperate to live. But the decision for him to die had already been made. As the saying goes, one cannot swap jokes with death, nor can one make deals with the *malach hamavet*, the angel of death.

I sought consolation and relief. But the methods accepted by American Jewish culture for easing my pain did not seem to address the questions I was asking. I needed insight that would lead me to wisdom. I was not looking for a promise of immortality exactly but for a dialogue that would address my deepest questions about life and death. Judaism, at least through the vehicle of the synagogue, seemed to offer only Bonds for Israel and reminders of a distant ethnicity.

But my stake in Judaism was strong. It was too ancient a path to have survived merely on lox and bagels. I was drawn to the visions that were repeated throughout the literature and occasionally in my heart. Visions, melodies whispered among the trees, the light of God shining in unexpected places—I hoped one of those places would be my soul.

But my visions, like all visions, were of short duration, a sharp flare of consciousness and insight. They were spice for the stew, but they could not serve as the meal itself. I knew I needed a guide. I needed someone who had walked a spiritual path and gained insight that he or she could share with me as I struggled with my grief.

Unfortunately I had great trouble finding teachers in the Jewish community who spoke to the spiritual nature of my concerns. Most of them were preoccupied with political or ethnic issues. Many could speak authoritatively only about the various laws of mourning. A fair number were numbed by the internecine politics of synagogue life. I would ask my questions and as often as not be steered in the direction of ancient writings, ancient words. These leaders seemed to be saying, "Let the ancient writings written by these holy but dead individuals guide you. I myself have no knowledge of what the hell you are talking about."

But I did not need more books. I was looking for the living power of the tradition. I needed not the description of the embrace of God but the actual, ongoing embrace itself. This was the desire that led me to India, and there I found teachers who introduced me to the practice of meditation. I began to experience the union with the Infinite that lies at the heart of all meditative practices, and I began to understand the difficulties and the rewards of committing myself to spiritual practice. But my search for answers was just beginning.

I knew that there were also Jewish teachers and teachings that had the power to illumine my grief and confusion with the pure and healing light of Torah. I had, in earlier years, already met a few such holy souls and had myself experienced miracles of clarity. But miracles are tricky things. They cannot really be clung to. They are a gift of the moment, like the insight of love. They can be transformative, but they cannot replace the hard work of striving for true wisdom. And this path of wisdom can only safely be pursued with the help of community and teachers.

The holy Ari, one of the greatest of the kabbalists, Jewish mystics, said that when he went walking, he saw the trees filled with souls calling and singing among the leaves. He mentioned this vision several times. The songs and words he heard uplifted him, but they did not replace the hard practice of life or the learning that took place with his teachers. His exalted visions were solidified and deepened by his immersion in the community of Sfat, a settlement of like-minded spiritual seekers.

My own search for a community within which to pursue my spiritual path began when I was quite young. In my early teens, I began to frequent a small, crumbling shul filled with old men and women—recent immigrants from Russia who spoke no English. They sported stainless steel teeth, which they chomped and flashed in ferocious smiles. They taught me a truncated Yiddish. I was never fluent, but the old men and women were eager for us to understand one another. They lived in a different world and wanted very much to introduce me to it. One old man proudly showed me his armless sleeve, neatly pinned to the shoulder. *"Ich gaherg asach Nazi!* I have killed many Nazis!" he cried. His eyes glinted like a rooster's.

These people were remnants of another Europe—hell, they were remnants of another planet. They held stories inside stories, visions locked inside larger visions. They spoke of alliances and passions for places that were deeper than I could imagine. They embodied loyalties that I in my exquisitely self-indulgent teens could barely fathom.

With the old men, I began to put on *t'fillin*, the small leather boxes filled with prayers and blessings that are worn on the upper arm and forehead during morning prayers; we gathered every morning—at 6:30 to be exact, which felt like the rising of the dead to me—and *davvened*, prayed, the morning service. The women brought schnapps, white cake, and creamed herring for a snack before we departed for home. They fussed over me and patted my cheeks—called me a *zisa kotchka*, a sweet duckling. Sometimes they would cry. Many of them had lived through the Holocaust. Understanding nothing, I would smile uneasily and hop on the bus. Arriving back home around 8:30, I would usually have to stare at the walls for a few minutes, drunk as a bug from the schnapps the old men had toasted me with. I was thirteen. It is a testament to my mother's great stamina and fortitude that this behavior didn't seem to worry her.

But later, as I grew older, these rituals were not enough. And when I began to experience the deepest pains of life, the pangs we call maturity, it was clear that I needed a teacher. Not a teacher of text, nor even a teacher of nostalgia, but a teacher of heart. One of the very few such people I met within the fractured Jewish world of those years appeared when I was nineteen. I had hitchhiked to New York (it was a different era, of course) with a tie-dyed yarmulke and T-shirt, looking to meet … whom? I did not have a clear idea; I only knew that I had a hunger, but it was not for bread, and that I thirsted, but not for water.

I walked up Williamsburg, which ran through the middle of the Chasidic neighborhood. The streets were crowded with baby carriages. Young and old men engaged in heated conversation, their hands waving excitedly. I stepped up to an old man who was strolling by himself and asked him in a garbled Yiddish-Hebrew-English mix where I could find a good bookstore. He was dressed in a long black frock coat, was slightly disheveled, and had a thick white beard that still held a trace of yellow from his youth. Nicotine stains wrestled in his mustache. His eyes were bright blue and not unfriendly.

He stepped back and eyed me up and down. I was a curious sight in my plumage of Jewish tie-dye. Deciding I was safe, he asked in a beautiful Yiddish mixed with a good bit of heavily accented English what I wanted.

"I would like to find a good bookstore," I repeated.

He started laughing. "A bookstore?!" he roared. "Don't you know, *yingele*, there is no end to books. You can fill great rooms with books, top to bottom. Books will not take you where you want to go."

"Then, what do I need, where do I need to go?" I squeaked.

He put his hand on my shoulder, suddenly serious. "You need community, my young friend," he said.

He told me many stories on that street corner, and we stood there until evening, talking. He told me of his life in Hungary and his departure during the fifties (very late for any Orthodox to be in that place). How despair had eaten at his heart when he came to this country and how he had contemplated suicide, so hard did it seem to be Jewish here.

At last we separated, he blessing me with a life filled with Torah and an early marriage filled with children.

I knew him as Mr. Schwartz. His answer to my first true questions, where should I go and what should I do, has proved more and more true over the years. In fact, his advice, I have come to understand, is the very essence of the Jewish path: work in tandem. Relationship, in all its varied forms—friends, family, teachers, and so on—is the ultimate guide.

Even meditation, in the Jewish tradition, is profoundly caught up in the realization of relationship. Whether one is meditating privately or praying with ten thousand at the Western Wall makes no difference. Relationship is a recurring manifestation of meditation.

When I returned from India, I was clear in my intention to follow a spiritual path. I was also determined to find authentic Jewish masters, however elusive they might be. It was not long after this that I met two Great Souls—Zalman Schachter-Shalomi and Shlomo Carlebach. These two men embodied all that is best in Judaism. Shlomo had an insightful story for every occasion and an irrepressible joy, and Zalman possessed the breadth of learning that continually commanded my attention. All of my future studies in Judaism returned ultimately to their strong beginning guidance.

Everything I write about in this book I have either seen or heard or experienced firsthand. In many modern Jewish circles, this approach is taboo; some folks prefer an academic, removed exposition of principles. But I agree with one of my teachers (Joe Miller, an itinerant Sufi, vaudevillian, and unschooled perfect master), who would sometimes quote, "It don't mean a thing if it ain't got that swing!" And then he would laugh uproariously.

In other words, unless a teaching comes from the heart, it is ultimately false. An early rebbe, a Jewish spiritual master, used to say that when he was first granted enlightenment, he decided at that very moment to transform the world. As time went on, though, he felt it best to bring enlightenment first to his town. Then, as the years passed, he realized perhaps he should concentrate on his family. Finally, he told his disciples, "I realized I had best work on myself. And I'm still at it." This focus on the personal is one of the distinguishing characteristics of Jewish meditation; for this reason, my own personal experiences form the basis of this book.

As my own journey has taught me, a spiritual life has no end; instead, it ever increases in richness. This is one of its promises. As we gain in *mochin gadlut*, Great Mind, we dip ever more deeply into the infinite well of joy that is God.

**CHAPTER I**

# Getting Our Bearings

*This teaching is not remote or*

*mysterious. It is not... across the sea*

*so [that you should] say, "Who will*

*cross the sea and get it for us, so*

*that we might be able to hear it*

*and keep it?" It is very close to you.*

*It is in your mouth and in your*

*heart so that you can fulfill it.*

Deuteronomy 30: 11-14

Many people have never heard of Jewish meditation and are surprised that there is such a thing. But meditation within the Jewish tradition has existed since biblical times. Immensely sophisticated, profuse in its techniques and lineages, it is alive and well—if still rather unknown.

Today, Jewish meditation is found mostly in the insular ultra-Orthodox world and within the more recent "renewal" movement. To understand why this is so—and why relatively few people have heard of Jewish meditation—we need to look at some historical facts. During the Second World War, just a little over fifty years ago, 30 to 40 percent of the Jewish people were killed. This fact is well known. But what is pertinent here is that 80 percent, perhaps as much as 90 percent, of the *traditional* community was destroyed. Lineages and schools that had been in existence since the Roman Empire were destroyed in thirty minutes. I have had teachers from Europe who taught hundreds of disciples of the first rank there, but none of these students survived the war. The destruction of these foundations of transmission resulted in widespread ignorance regarding the Kabbalah, Jewish spirituality, and Jewish meditation and contemplative practice.

The Jewish community has spent the years since the *Shoah*, the Holocaust, growing a new spiritual heart. Slowly, the teachers who survived have spread their teachings and in turn created new teachers. Some of the meditational disciplines they have passed along have been reconstructed by students who were not yet masters, and although this has created a few false starts and some misdirection, it has also given rise to tremendous energy and enthusiasm. Many of the teachers today teach the time-honored substance of the faith yet also understand the questions asked by modern students, for these teachers inevitably inhabit both worlds.

Judaism is an ancient path. It is the oldest continuously held and transmitted tradition on the planet. Many of the mystic and meditative traditions of Christianity and Islam arise out of it. Indeed, Judaism was already middle-aged when Buddhism was born. This is in no way meant to denigrate these other spiritualities. All paths lead to the *Echad*, the One. But it is important to grasp the immense longevity of the Torah path. One of my young students once brought a history text over to my house. In it was a long section on the birth of Mesopotamian civilization and the rise of the city-states of Ur and Chaldea. He was shocked when I told him that the Jewish people had arisen at the same time as, and possibly even earlier than, these ancient cities. Our age gives us some perspective. It has also provided us with a tremendous wealth of learning and vast oceans of insight.

During this long history, many meditative techniques have arisen within Judaism—far too many to describe within the practical length of one book or even a hundred like it. My intention here is to provide a brief general outline and guide to the Jewish tradition of meditation. This tradition is approachable by all interested seekers, not just Jews. Of course I write from my own perspective, but I also draw heavily on the teachings of academics like Gershom Scholem, Rivka Schatz-Uffenheimer, Moshe Idel, Daniel Matt,[1] and many others whose importance cannot be overestimated. And I am indebted to practitioners like Aryeh Kaplan, Rebbe Zalman Schachter-Shalomi, Jonathan Omer-Man, David Cooper,[2] and others for their insight into both the practice of Jewish meditation and its theoretic underpinnings. Ultimately, a practice is not an academic exercise. It has its own life, its own breath. This is the most important thing to understand.

There are vast differences among the various Jewish meditational and spiritual practices. Some are very active, while others are profoundly calm and still. A practice (referred to in Hebrew as an *avodah*) is ultimately meant to liberate us and provide insight into the structuring and unfolding of reality. But the ways in which we reach such vision vary enormously. The Talmud says, "Look how great is God! A person who makes coins, each one is identical. But God, each person is the same yet each one is a separate world!" This is also true of Jewish meditation. There are many schools of thought, many coins, all with the same intent and yet distinct in practice. If you are not satisfied with one school or teacher, you can step aside and find another.

# The Origins of Jewish Meditation

Jewish meditation has its roots, not surprisingly, in the Bible. The Torah itself (the first five books of the Bible) is replete with references to meditation. But the origins of Jewish meditation are even easier to trace (and the tradition more completely spelled out) in the books of the prophets. In Hebrew, a prophet is called a *navi.* Practitioner Aryeh Kaplan pointed out that this word has three etymologies. One is *navach* (to cry out), another is *nava* (to gush, to flow forth), and the last is *navuv* (to be hollow). All three etymologies help us understand biblical meditation and its relationship to prophecy and enlightenment. For the prophet was as one hollow, his or her ego stripped away. The prophet was the flute through which flowed the Infinite One's wind and melody.

There is another important point to be gathered from looking at the prophets: Although the prophets, as well as other early archetypal figures such as Sarah and Abraham, were clearly enlightened, this achievement did not lessen their responsibilities to the community. The ongoing responsibility of *tikkun olam* (repairing or healing the world) has always been a fundamental part of Jewish spiritual practice. From generation to generation this belief has, if anything, only deepened. Early teachers often put themselves in psychic and physical danger through their meditative ascents, entering realms far beyond what we normally think of as simple *mochin gadlut* (enlightenment). But they did this always in order to hurry the great healing (the *tikkun olam*); they were seeking to "hurry the Messiah" for the benefit of the world.

This mixture of social responsibility and mystical achievement is characteristic of the Torah path. A person's enlightenment cannot be measured outside of his or her relationship with friends, lovers, peers, children, and community. There is an old expression: "If you want to know the spiritual attainment of your teacher, ask their spouse"—in other words, ask someone who sees them with their hair down. In the Jewish tradition, neither teachers nor prophets can easily be removed from their various social contexts or from the great social concerns of their time. The Book of Micah states it simply: "Shall I come before him with burnt offerings ... with ten thousand rivers of oil? ... [You know] what is good and what the Lord requires of you—Do justice and love kindness."[3] Enlightenment without compassion and concern for righteousness is at best naive, at worst a venue for oppression. A Jewish understanding of enlightenment requires that one not remove himself or herself from the needs and concerns of the many. This understanding is found in the most ancient traditions of the Torah path, and it continues today. The prophets (like the later Chasidic masters) lived in communal situations, not in monastic retreats, and therefore they had numerous cultural obligations. The importance of these familial and cultural relationships is somewhat hard to grasp for most moderns who are on a spiritual path, but it is crucial for an accurate understanding of Jewish meditation and enlightenment.

But what was the actual practice of Jewish meditation like in the beginning? Biblical references suggest that the ancient tradition used several means to elevate the meditator, and one of them was music. Music served as a way to focus the meditator's mind, helping her[4] to pass through the illusions of everyday consciousness and elevate her thoughts. The Baal Shem Tov, the founder of Chasidism, taught, "Through music you can reach joy and union with the Infinite One.[5]

From its origins, Jewish meditation has held that music has the power to heal and redeem. Our own experience confirms this. We sing the blues to lighten our hearts. We whistle while we work. In Jerusalem I watched an old man, bent over with age and rheumatism, shuffle onto the dance floor during the festival of Simchat Torah (the rejoicing of the law), pick up the scroll of the law (a good forty-pound weight), and begin to dance with it. He circled slowly, but as he moved his body straightened, his steps became lighter, until he was whirling with the Torah held high above his head. His face was a flame, and he moved like a torch across the room.

# Judaism and Other Paths

Judaism is a path that focuses on the particular rather than on the universal. It tends to concern itself with the close, the familial, and the intimate, rather than with the abstract, the far, and the impersonal. In this it is similar to all tribal religions. It stresses the individual—especially the need for individuals to reflect on themselves and their actions in the world—but it is best and most accurately viewed as a communal vision. Individuality is conceived only within the womb of the tribe. In other words, only by surrendering to the needs of the group—and, by extension, to the will of God—can one's true individuality be found.

In contrast, Buddhism and Christianity arise from the grace of the perfect enlightenment of one individual: Buddha and Jesus, respectively. In Buddhism especially, this has resulted in a theological system of great coherence. The Four Noble Truths and the Eightfold Path are simple and logical. But the fact that the Buddha was a monastic and Jesus a renunciate, each renouncing aspects of the world, has affected the subsequent forms these paths have taken as well as their teachings concerning spiritual practice. Though in both Christianity and Mahayana Buddhism it is believed that grace can eventually come to all creatures, both emphasize *individual* practice and monastic discipline.

The spiritual and meditative path of Judaism, on the other hand—even at its most personal and individual—is forever harking back to its collective and tribal root by its emphasis on family, intimacy, and tribe. This is one reason why the Jewish spiritual path as a whole (and Jewish meditation specifically) is very broad and seemingly untidy. Exactly *because* it is familial and intimate, valuing the close and the personal, it is messy, gossipy, homey—it is the path of heart, which always implies the potential for soreness and contradiction.

So while it is true that Jewish *avodah* is still a matter of individual will, the matrix in which that will is practiced stems from a very different consciousness than do the great universalistic religions of Islam, Buddhism, or Christianity. Buddhism, for example, emphasizes universal laws. These laws are usually called the dharma, and they seek to explain how the world behaves and moves. For Buddhists, the image that best describes the world's natural movement is the ebb and flow of the tides. Judaism, by contrast, is a particularistic path, focusing on the personal and the intimate.

If we tried to come up with a central Jewish metaphor to capture the way of the world, it might be Chinese boxes. There is ebb and flow, but this flux, like a box within a box, resides within stability, and that stability in turn resides within flux, which resides within stability, and so on. The central point—the end of the boxes, as it were—is the *Ayn Sof*: the Without-End, the infinite point of zero. The *Ayn Sof* is the heart of wisdom and the center of all being. It is depicted kabbalistically as the pure white light, the diamond light. But even in the place of *Ayn Sof* there is intimacy; there is an eye that sees, an ear that hears, and a heart that feels.

But there are also places where the Jewish path coincides with those of other spiritual traditions. When we talk about the nature of karma, for instance, we speak about a general and ultimately exact reciprocity: "What goes around comes around." There is something in the soul of our species that gravitates toward the notion of balance, of harmony. These concepts are fundamental to almost all religious paths, including Buddhism, Islam, Christianity, and, of course, Judaism.

Now, in some paths, balance and harmony are viewed almost mechanistically, as in the way a weighted boat will always right itself. Balance is seen as a law of nature, not a *personal* thing. But in the Jewish path, balance is profoundly personal. The balance of the world arises from the well of compassion and mercy *(chesed* and *rachamim)* that is centered in what we call God— the force of infinite love that gives rise to the universe and establishes the world. Compassion, mercy, love—these are all personal attributes; in fact, they are the very bonds that link human beings in relationship. Thus, these attributes form the heart of Jewish spiritual practice. Meditation in the Jewish path means developing more intimacy with the divine in every aspect of life—in our simple day-to-day actions as well as when we are sunk in deep prayer.

The point of this discussion is not to say that one view is right and another wrong; it is simply to point out that there are clear differences among these spiritualities both in the underlying focus of each and, as a result, in the paths they offer the spiritual seeker.

# The Task of Meditation

In every tradition, meditation is a way of focusing the consciousness in order to break through to a new level of understanding or being. In Judaism, the task of meditation is specifically to open the heart, to unclog the channel between the Infinite and the mortal. For the meditator, "the soul becomes a throne for the Supernal Light above the head ... and the light spreads around him and he is within the light, sitting and trembling with joy."[6] This union with the Infinite is the most important thing. All of the *mitzvot* (spiritual practices) are ultimately designed to further this rapturous attachment (*devekut*). Even the practice of sitting and studying holy texts, so prized in the yeshiva world, is aimed at this union. However, when the study of the texts gets in the way of actually experiencing God, the texts should be given a rest.

The Jewish medieval philosopher Luzzatto taught that the ultimate task is *"ha adam mashlim et atzmo"*; (a person should perfect himself or herself). The ultimate perfection of ourselves lies in union with the Infinite, which is often called *bitul hayesh*—literally, "annihilation of that which is."

In turn, the Mezritcher rebbe, the leader of the Chasidic movement in the early 1700s, taught that not a thing in the world can change from one reality into another unless it first turns into *nothing*—which is the in-between stage of things. This way of defining union with the Infinite has continued to gain credence among most of the modern meditation teachers I know. The Mezritcher rebbe postulated that one can stay in this in-between stage or move solidly into the universe of "things" while still maintaining a heart of nothingness. This place of nothing (called *ayin)* is in fact what sustains all physical reality.

But one must give oneself over to this *ayin*, this infinite Nothing. This is the primary goal of spiritual practice. But such a giving over of one's self can be very frightening and difficult. There is a teaching: "When we become aware that only God exists, then God receives from us the complete joy he hopes for."[7] This expresses two pivotal points. First, there is only God, by which we mean the Oneness that subsumes all categories. We might call this Oneness the ocean of reality and everything that swims in it. "Only God exists"—this teaching is itself a wonderful and ancient meditation. It is the first admonition of the *eseret hadibrot*, the Ten Commandments. Ultimately, no matter where we are in our level of perception, there is only *zot*, thisness. *Zot* is a feminine word for "this." The word *zot* is itself one of the names of God—the *thisness* of what is.

Second, the essence of God is *chesed*, a joyful compassion. In retrospect it was the hunger for union with God on this level—*chesed*—that drove me, when I was twenty-three, to India. I wanted to feel more of that joyful compassion. I wanted to be filled with it. And since I couldn't seem to find it in America, I traveled to India. I lived in a little village called Ashapur, near Benares. Benares is the Jerusalem of India, and I spent a lot of time there. Bodies are taken to Benares and burned on the ghats, the stone steps leading to the Ganges, with the expectation that this will ensure a higher reincarnation.

Night is never silent in that place. Prayer bells and conch horns bellow like sobbing gods. Incense, lit to honor the corpses, fills the air like millions of slightly rank orchids. And of course, underlying this, there is always the smell of meat. I sat on the red sandstone steps with Buddhist priests and Hindu sadhus, wandering holy renunciates. We talked of Petrarch and dentures, Macy's Christmas sales, Upanishadic liberation, and simple survival. Even in such matters as nirvana, we live in an age of the eclectic. The information revolution has annihilated innocence. Yak herders leaf through catalogs and inquire anxiously about the Dow Jones or the revolution in Mexico. Nomads are concerned with the price of gasoline in San Jose. Every Sikh taxi driver has a cousin in Chicago or Nairobi or Singapore. And why not? But for me at the time this profusion of stimuli only exacerbated my restlessness and dissatisfaction.

I had come to India depressed, heartsick, looking for answers. And I found answers—of a sort. But I was learning that such answers demand action; otherwise they have no meaning. I had begun to meditate, but that alone was not enough. For if meditation is to open us to the Infinite, it requires from us a commitment—the commitment of time and energy. We must give back if we hope to receive. For me this truth was hard to accept. Taking on a spiritual discipline can be daunting, but the rewards far outweigh the difficulties. Distractions abound, but if we can keep our focus in spite of all the stimuli we are bombarded with, meditation will yield a great return—which we may call, for want of a better word, God.

# Modern Definitions of Jewish Meditation

Within the long Jewish tradition, meditation has taken various forms or styles. Today, some teachers divide Jewish meditation into three main types. The first type is *structured, externally directed* meditation. Meditations of this type are generally called *hitbonenut* meditations. The idea is to contemplate an object, using it to attain a higher level of consciousness. *Hitbonenut* meditations are also generally "mental" meditations. Today, among Jews in both the United States and Israel, there is a lot of emphasis on the mind; contemplation and concentration are used almost as synonyms. Chabad, or Lubavitch, a Chasidic group based in New York that derives its style of meditation from a text called the Tanya, is a classic system that embraces the *hitbonenut* meditations of a very mental variety.

Meditation of this first type is called "external" because the meditator contemplates an "outside" object—a mantra, a candle flame, a written word, a sentence from the Torah. The mind is directed toward the liberation of spirit not by concentrating on what arises within itself but by focusing on a thing. This type of meditation is considered "structured" because it is repeated daily and follows the same outline each time.

The second type is *inner directed.* These meditations are sometimes called *hitbodedut.* The meditator focuses inward, watching the thoughts and feelings that arise internally. These meditations are often silent, but they do not have to be. While the mind contemplates the play of its own self, the mouth may give utterance to any spontaneous words of prayer and glorification that arise. Rebbe Nachman's conversations with

God (in the eighteenth century) are often used as an example *of hitbodedut.* This type of meditation is aimed at strengthening the power of *ahavah* (love) by focusing on the *Boreh Baruch Hu* (the Creator, blessed is he!), as God is found within the soul of every person. In other words, it involves giving oneself over to a spontaneous outpouring of love.

The third type of meditation may be thought of as being essentially *nondirected.* This method seeks to enter the *Ayn Sof* without the use of metaphor or of a "ladder" of ascent. It seeks to be united with the One in an instant rather than through a gradual process. In a very real sense, all of these meditations seek this state of Oneness, but nondirected meditation (the contemplation of the *Ayn Sof* itself) is without frills or a helping hand. It seeks the direct route with no detours. It is sudden insight. This is a difficult technique to describe, since the instant we use words we are no longer dwelling on the *Ayn Sof* but have entered dual consciousness. Suffice it to say that the technique revolves around the contemplation of nothingness. This assumes different forms in each person's practice, and only practice can perfect it. For example, one sits and places consciousness towards the state that seems like *Ayn Sof.* Within a few moments some emotion or thought will intrude. Immediately, consciousness is placed again into *Ayn Sof.* This is a very difficult and tiring technique and should be done only with a teacher.

Though Kaplan and some other teachers divide Jewish meditation into these three main types, I tend to simplify these distinctions. I believe that all types of meditation fall into two broad categories that I call "pushing" and "releasing," which I will define in the next section. But even these two categories are not so distinct; they tend to blur and blend in actual practice. The mind is a fitful, dancing, wild thing. When we meditate, our efforts are aimed not so much at subduing the mind as at directing it. A meditation practice must be flexible enough to accomplish this, and the meditator should not be overly concerned with the exact name and history of this or that technique.

# Stages of Meditation

When I am teaching, I often divide the types of Jewish meditation into two simple categories: *Pushing* meditation is one in which the mind is being used actively; in a *releasing* meditation the mind is being released. One could also divide Jewish meditations according to whether they lead the meditator in *a gradual ascent* or provide *sudden insight.* A brief review of Jewish meditational practices helps to clarify these distinctions.

According to Aryeh Kaplan, most meditation up through kabbalistic times followed a primary order. First, the meditator enters a *hagah* meditation—that is, an externally directed contemplation. The meditator directs her consciousness to a point outside herself. She quiets her mind by repeating a melody, word, sound, and so on until she comes close to a state of *bitul*, ego annihilation. Talmud describes this ascent using the metaphor of chambers or palaces. This might be thought of as a gradually ascending meditation. It is also what I call a pushing meditation in that the mind is actively engaged.

As the meditator moves higher in her mind, she enters a *siyach* meditation, which consists of a pointed releasing of the mind into one of the palaces, or transcendental realms. *Siyach* meditation is an active wiping clean of the mind. Its name comes from the same root as "to wipe off." It is generally a pushing meditation because the mind actively moves itself in ascent. Its variant is *suach*, from the root "to smooth." This stresses tranquillity where one may mentally "float" up or not, as the meditative condition mandates. The *suach* variant is a releasing type of meditation. It does not require pushing.

The *hagah* and *siyach* meditations are sometimes collapsed together and called "entering the *pardes*, garden." This is a very physical and visual meditation. The body may sweat, twitch, and experience panic. The mind may begin to envision a kaleidoscopic flow of images, some soothing, some terrifying. The Talmud cautions against the dangers of this form of meditation. There is a story that illustrates its dangers; it goes like this: Four sages entered the garden. One died, one went mad, one became a heretic, and one entered in peace and left in peace.

As a student becomes more advanced, his meditation often progresses from a single-pointed *kavannah*, a passionate intentionality concerning the meditation, to a mindlessness *kavannah*; that is, intentionality is still present, but there is little or no ego underpinning it. Both "pushing" and "releasing" types of meditation can lead the meditator here. This provides an entry into nothingness. This stage is called *bitul*, or *bitul hayesh*, annihilation of what is. Dov Ber said, "Think of yourself as Nothing *(ayin)* and forget yourself totally. Then you can transcend time ... where all is equal: life and death, ocean and dry land."[8] This is one of the highest stages of an ordinary enlightenment. This state may be entered during stationary meditation, but with practice one can proceed until it includes all of one's life—in other words, one is *bitul* while diapering the baby or driving the car.

All of these are methods of gradual ascent. Also common, though, is the idea that enlightenment can be attained much more directly. Any breakthrough of consciousness has the potential to unlock numerous doors of *mochin*, mind. For example, a breakthrough in consciousness concerning the quality of compassion or generosity— or even the performance of the simple acts that we do from one moment to the next—has the potential to unlock other doors of spiritual perception. Alexander Susskind, an eighteenth-century teacher, urged us, "When you eat and drink, you experience enjoyment and pleasure from the food and drink. Arouse yourself every moment to ask in wonder, 'What is this enjoyment and pleasure? What is it that I am tasting?'"[9] These breakthroughs are moments of sudden insight, which may come about regardless of the meditation style or technique one is using. Each insight offers the potential for immediate breakthrough to the Infinite One.

But it is always up to the individual to imbue every meditation—indeed, every action—with heart and not permit any aspect of life to be merely rote. Whether the student's practice consists of sudden insight or gradual ascent, whether it includes pushing or releasing meditation, the Jewish path expects the student to continue her *avodah* through the activities of her daily life (such as eating and working) and to turn the tools of meditation, such as self-awareness, consistently on herself; she cannot expect the technique of, say, merely visualizing the Hebrew name of God to do the work for her. Technique is only effective up to a point. No technique in and of itself will bring understanding.

# Reassembling the Fragments

This, then, is the broad state of the Jewish spiritual and meditation world today. Disjointed, personal, fractured, filled with the past, passionate about the future, it is experiencing a great reawakening of creativity. Shattered, traumatized by the near total destruction of our spiritual heritage, the Jewish vision is again beginning to offer itself as a viable path of personal practice for tens of thousands of individuals. Slowly, like mercury, the pieces of Jewish contemplative practice are reassembling themselves. Here and there, quickly and slowly, back and forth, the teachings arise again. Among the sadhus of India, I experienced some of the teachings (albeit phrased differently) of the Mezritcher rebbe — not the least of them being, if you want the fruit you've got to water the roots. Jewish spiritual teachings are so deep and so profoundly needed by the world that there is no choice but that they will again be disseminated to all who are ready to receive them. But the most important place where this spiritual message can resurface is in you. Each reader, each person, precious beyond words—the teaching must surface in your heart. teachings arise again. Among the sadhus of India, I experienced some of the teachings (albeit phrased differently) of the Mezritcher rebbe— not the least of them being, if you want the fruit you've got to water the roots. Jewish spiritual teachings are so deep and so profoundly needed by the world that there is no choice but that they will again be disseminated to all who are ready to receive them. But the most important place where this spiritual message can resurface is in you. Each reader, each person, precious beyond words—the teaching must surface in your heart.

# Refelection on the Interrelationship of All Things

Whether you have meditated before or are just beginning, it is always valuable to come to your practice as though for the first time. Try to approach this meditation without too much expectation. You are just going to let the meditation unfold at its own rate, so don't be in a rush.

Find a comfortable place where you can sit quietly for fifteen to thirty minutes. It should be a place where you feel safe and where you won't be disturbed. Evening is the best time for this type of meditation. You may want to close your eyes. Focus first on your breaking, breaking deeply and regularly and allowing yourself to become calm and centered. As you continue to breathe in this relaced way, imagine yourself at the center of a circle. Around you are seated your relatives and friends. Try to visualize them very clearly in your mind's eye. Acknowledge all aspects—both positive and negative—

of your relationships to them, for each relationship is part of what makes you you.

Now expand this circle, adding co-workers and acquaintances. Again, acknowledge your relationships to these people. Then expand the circle again, including the Jewish people or the members of your own spiritual group. What is your relationship to them? Then expand it again to include the people in your town.

Now take yourself out of the center and place yourself within that great circle. Reflect that you are simply part of an ever-expanding circle in which each person is connected to the others. You may, if you wish, begin to add animals and plants, soil and sea to the circle, or you may wish to keep it fixed only on humans. Either way is fine.

As you do this exercise, certain questions may arise. These questions may include:

What is the connection between myself and a distant being?

Does this connection give me strength or weaken me?

Can I surrender to the knowledge that I am related to all these souls?

Listen quietly for answers, but do not demand them. Not every exercise or meditation brings immediate answers. Simply relax and try to hear or feel how your body, your mind, and your emotions are responding to the exercise.

When you are ready, open your eyes. Then, as you go about your daily activities, pay attention to your thoughts and feelings about your relationships as they are actually played out. Try to notice how the experience of this exercise is reflected in your daily life. Remember that there is no right or wrong here and that understanding comes at its own pace. Some things really cannot be hurried.

# CHAPTER 2

# Learning Some Basic Concepts

*There was once a prudish, angry old man who never had any fun. He would not even let his cat out to have a good time. Finally, he decided to go to Los Angeles. Before he went, he told his caretaker to keep the cat indoors. But once in L.A., he got caught up in a great love affair that carried him on wings of joy from event to event. After a week of this, he faxed his caretaker "Having a hell of a time!" he wrote. "Let the cat out!"*

By its nature religion is meant to let the cat out. It is meant to open the door of our soul to the sweetness of God and the world. In spite of the many differences of opinion within the Jewish path and the many divisions among teachers and philosophies, this is its main teaching.

This chapter looks at the basic concepts that underlie Jewish spirituality and thus form the foundation for a Jewish meditation practice. First we will look at the two main branches of the Torah path; then we will talk about the central importance of engaging the heart in our practice, as in our lives. This leads us to the personal and communal nature of the Torah path and to the acts of blessing and healing as a means of elevating our daily lives. Finally, in the light of all these basic principles, we will look again at meditation itself and at how it supports the joyful awareness that lies at the heart of the Jewish path.

# The Paths of Torah

One of the fundamental principles of Judaism is that Torah can be transmitted only through relationship with the Infinite One. But there are two broad methods, or paths, by which this relationship is learned and passed on: the path of passion (or heart) and the path of mind. Basically, I teach according to the path of passion and heart. Both ways are time honored, and neither one is better than the other; which path one chooses is more a matter of what kind of music one responds to. The same melody is not for everyone.

The passionate path advocates a practice that builds an *emotional* relationship with the Infinite. This path is sometimes called *hitlahavut*—the way of flame. Those who take the mental path, on the other hand, seek primarily to understand and accumulate learning. For example, the members of Chabad, a school of intellectual Chasidim believe that "contemplative prayer is very much a severe intellectual exercise, in which emotional rapture … must follow on contemplation but not be a part of it."[1] In other words, the followers of Chabad enthusiastically assume that the power of mind will eventually lead the individual to joy in God's infinite process. Unceasing study of the Talmud is a technique hallowed by the Jewish tradition and adhered to by large numbers of Jewish people.

The path of heart perceives the nature of the Infinite through the lens of intimacy and personalness. God is father, mother, brother, friend, lover, God. The holy Zohar, one of the main books of Jewish mysticism, asserts that God and the Torah are one, by which it means that if you look deeply enough, there is no separation between the mystical and the concrete. One may make this realization gradually, or one may swallow it in one gulp (to paraphrase an old Zen saying). The passionate practice attempts to perceive the universe *all together*—blood, bone, and spirit. This intimate path is through the heart and the senses. It perceives the Infinite through the driving principle of the universe, which is *chesed*, or loving-kindness. The path of heart suffuses us with the love of the universe and of all creation that inhabits it, for all of creation is organically connected. Moses De Leon, the probable writer of the Zohar, said, "Everything is linked with everything else down to the lowest ring on the chain, and the true essence of God is above as well as below, in the Heaven and on the Earth, and nothing exists outside of Him."[2] The path of heart asks us to see this connection in an *intimate* rather than an abstract or distant way. And so we learn to see this totality (which we call God) reflected in the very finiteness, close-upness, and personalness of our lives.

The passionate path teaches that the heart of the universe hears our pleas and has compassion for us. We do not need to worry about whether there is a *God* in the world; we need only realize that the universe is filled with *godliness.* When we recognize this, we become able to receive God's love—and to love in return. We put ourselves in a state of total reciprocity. Rebbe Levi Yitzhak of Berditchev used to teach, "When God wishes to bestow good, we must be able to accept it. It is God's nature constantly to bestow His love upon us.... When we put ourselves in a state where we can accept God's good, this is His delight."[3] And it is our delight, too.

The mental path, by contrast, places an enormous emphasis on textual study. This is the route taken by much of modern Orthodoxy, including the ultra-Orthodox and Chasidim. It is sometimes called *Torah lishma*, or Torah for its own sake. In an ideal setting, this approach is an excellent one. For just as doing *zazen*, Zen sitting meditation, only for its own sake and not for the sake of enlightenment can actually lead to enlightenment, so, too, the all-consuming discipline of Torah study, by relaxing the mind, has the potential to yield tremendous spiritual fruit.

However, because this is a textually based sensibility, it can sometimes degenerate into mere sophistry—even as the path of heart can degenerate into debauchery. When either of these things happens, the soul that hungers is left without nourishment; it is removed from the source of joy. It is as though the people who are hungry for spiritual food are given only a menu to eat. Every emphasis, every possible path in spirituality, has a potential dark side. We should always be aware of this while not allowing ourselves to become unduly burdened by it. The most important thing is to persevere. Ultimately, all that is required is that we hear the music and join the dance. Sometimes, on any path, this is very simple, sometimes very difficult.

But the end result, the goal (to the extent that these two approaches have goals), is essentially the same. Ultimately it is *echad*: unity, oneness. The paths offer different gates. None is ultimately more correct. The Kabbalah at one point describes the Jewish path as a candle in a room of mirrors. This is very apt. There are a thousand doorways. Each one works. The most difficult thing is deciding which one works best for you.

# Engaging the Heart

If we choose the path of heart, then of course our focus is ultimately and always on love. Love is the cornerstone of many of the world's religions, especially the mystic paths. Rebbe Nachman of Bratslav used to say that achieving the simplicity of love is one of the highest enlightenments. The attainment of true loving-kindness is the cornerstone of Jewish practice. Often this comes easily; the sluice of the heart is opened and the water flows. But some of the gates of the heart are closed, and these can be opened only through a strong spiritual practice.

Our experience of loving-kindness fills us with joy; in fact, according to the Torah, joy is the normal healthy state of the soul. When I was a child, I had a set of Punch-and-Judy dolls— those large, child-sized dolls with the rounded bottoms that always return them to an upright position regardless of how often you knock them down. Our soul, too, has a rounded base, which always returns us to the state of *chesed*, no matter how often we are knocked down.

*Chesed* can be translated as loving-kindness, though it is an active word rather than a passive one. I tend to translate it as something like "joyful compassion" or "ecstatic compassion" or "compassionate joyful love." No phrase is quite adequate in English. *Chesed* does not necessarily involve a Hare-Krishna-style ecstatic jumping around (though there is nothing wrong with this); rather, it generally refers to what happens when we experience the connection between the soul and the reality of God. When the joining of these two is acknowledged, the heart swells with *chesed*, and every part of creation feels this swell. Here is how the psalm describes it: "The heavens exclaim God's glory, the sky affirms.... Day speaks to day and night to night. There is silence, there are no words—But their voices resonate throughout the earth!"[4]

When we speak of the heart, which is the lens of *chesed*, of course we speak of love. Love is the doorway to the soul. It is the consuming wisdom that arises when a person is connected to the source. It is the melody Nachman described as filling every leaf, every stone. Part of our task in meditation is to learn to hear this melody—and the more we hear it, the deeper it will resonate in our soul. The *chesed* that underpins the world is boundless. It is the very fabric of the world. This is reflected in the root word for love in Hebrew: *A-H-V.* Normally we pronounce this word as *ahavah*, but the grammar of Hebrew (which is without vowels) permits us to break it down into two words: *eh-hav*, meaning "I will give." And love is being given constantly, though we may be closed to it.

Most of the discipline of Jewish practice is aimed at helping the student fall in love. This is the passionate way. The Talmud tells a story of a great master who went home and began making love with his wife. Suddenly he realized someone was under his bed! "Who's there?" he cried.

"It is me," responded one of his students.

"What the hell are you doing?" shouted the master.

"This, too, is Torah; I must learn it as well," responded the eager disciple.

The Talmud does not relate how the master responded to this quick-witted fellow; no doubt he threw the rascal out. But he might also have embraced him. For the disciple was following the spark; he realized that everything depends on the flame of the heart.

Once, after I gave a talk, someone from the audience asked me to sum up this passionate path of heart that I kept talking about. I responded with an old Chasidic parable. "Imagine a forge," I said. "This represents your practice. Now imagine the worker with his tools. This is you and your intention. But what is lacking? Only a spark. This is the path of *chesed*, to ignite the spark that gets the whole forge going. Without it the forge remains cold." The path and the exercises in this book, then, aim at igniting the spark, feeling the joy of *chesed.*

I have sometimes heard Buddhism described as the way of the quiet pool or of the moonlit garden. The Jewish way is the way of the wave, crashing and laughing; it is the way of flame.

# The Personal and Communal Nature of Torah

When we begin to learn the Torah way, we notice right away the numerous mentions of God. For many Americans the notion of God is very difficult; it is not a concept that has much meaning for many of us. Perhaps we think of a large man with a beard and a bad temper. This difficulty is compounded by the paucity of English words that denote God. In everyday language we use four or five words for God: Lord, Father, Mother, God … and that's about it. In Hebrew, Aramaic, Yiddish, and Ladino (the common languages of Jewish God-talk), there are easily forty or fifty words for the ever-changing notion of God. God may be expressed as a verb as easily as it is as a noun. God may be thought of as a process rather than as an entity.

But even when we have made our peace with our own sense of God, the spirituality found in the Torah, while superficially easy to understand, may be difficult to grasp: there are all those men and women bashing each other, and a Supreme Being who seems perpetually either very angry or very happy!

Grasping this mystery is key to all of Jewish spirituality and to the discipline of meditation. All of Torah is based on the idea of relationship and intimacy. The language of the Torah is wildly anthropomorphic, but the *purpose* of anthropomorphism is to bring us into closer contact with the Infinite, to give us a sense of the *personal*. The Torah's anthropomorphic language is very different from the language of Buddhist sutras and of the Hindu Upanishads, which are very logical and impersonal in tone. The Torah's truth lies in its simple, unassuming stories and speech. Corey Fisher of the Traveling Jewish Theatre once said that the world is not made up of atoms but of stories. Indeed it is. This is a profound insight into the entire manner by which Torah and *mochin gadlut* are transmitted in the Jewish tradition. The force of the Infinite is found in the simple contexts of life, not in high, philosophical revelations. *Ayn Sof* can best be possessed when we are at our most human—that is, at our most intimate. Not when we have limited our palette of human response and emotion but when we have expanded it are we able to access *Ayn Sof.*

This brings us back to the experience of joy that is central to the way of flame. Joy is by its nature forever in the present. When we are very happy, we are usually not very aware of the past or the future. We are in the eternal now. But to cultivate this presentness requires a responsibility to the past and the future. Every creature we have encountered and every occurrence we have experienced are with us always. Ultimately there is no forgetting and no leaving behind. Thus, our own past and the Jewish tradition combine to ground us in a communal, familial setting, and it is this communal context that gives us the strength to be in the (often difficult) present.

This brings us round again to the foundation stone of the Jewish path: Even in the furthest reaches of enlightenment, even in the furthest reaches of the Infinite, there is the personal. The personal exists in community and family; hence these disciplines are stressed as part of the spiritual path. Development of intimacy with all things is the essence of the Torah.

# Blessing and Healing in the Jewish Path

ne of the ways in which this intimacy is both discovered and expressed is through the process of blessing and being blessed. The Jewish path, in fact, is sometimes called the Blessing Way.

What does it mean to bless and be blessed? It means, first of all, to be aware of each act that we do. To our awareness of each act, we add joy. As we bring joy to our mind and actions, we break through to the awareness that every bit of God's creation is blessed and that when we partake of it we also are blessed. So we make a blessing on even our simplest acts or objects—an item of food or drink or apparel—in order to strengthen our awareness of universal blessing. We begin to see how simple things such as eating or drinking, helping a friend, providing hospitality, visiting a scholar, or forgiving an enemy are, in turn, blessed by God. And so our consciousness is elevated so that we ourselves *feel* blessed by joy, wonder, splendor, and peace. And to feel blessed is to be perpetually reborn. This is summed up by an old song line that I have always found to be a great Torah: "He not busy being born is busy dying."

As our awareness of blessing grows, so does our joy. When we bless something, we center our attention on a very holy moment, for the power of blessing will tend to focus our mind, regardless of where it may have been wandering. We are brought to joy. And through this joy in our practice, we are finally brought to ultimate joy. This is the ladder by which enlightenment is gained.

Like blessing, healing is a major component of the Jewish path. *Tikkun olam*, healing the world, is cited as being one of the obligations with which we are born. Though the world is conceived as being good in all its aspects, there is also the notion that it is dynamic, and as a dynamic structure, it is always in need of repair. This is where the soul of humanity comes in. It is our duty to make this repair, which is best accomplished by the quality of mercy and *chesed* that we give back to creation. We bless the world around us in order to heal it.

"Healing" may be defined in the traditional sense of curing or making well, but it can be understood in a deeper way as elevating the task or condition at hand. To "elevate" a task or condition means that we focus our intention and dedicate our experience of it to the higher purpose of the Infinite. We give over the experience to the Infinite, recognizing that "whatever happens to you happens because God wants it to happen."[5] This acknowledgment is a very forceful and difficult method of destroying the ego, for it requires relinquishing control of the experience and its outcome.

The experience of pain is a good example. Many people assume that because they are experiencing pain they must have done something wrong. They confuse responsibility and fault. It is good to take responsibility, but between responsibility and fault there lies an abyss. The universe consists of wheels within wheels, and we can make ourselves crazy trying to understand all its complexities. Elevating the experience of pain, giving it over to the purposes of the Infinite One, helps us to let go of this mental dilemma. The more we can do this, the more we enter the universe of *bitul*, ego annihilation. The process of elevating is a simple and practical tool to be used in our daily practice, and in fact, the most common teaching of the Jewish path is that we should elevate our day-to-day tasks. By becoming aware of each moment and giving it over to the Infinite, we bring ourselves close to it. We become, as it were, intimate with each moment, even with what pains us. And so we arrive at true wisdom. As the great master Dov Baer used to say, "The sense of closeness is the attribute of wisdom."

Blessing and healing bring us into intimate relationship with the Infinite and thus bring us closer to *mochin gadlut*, Great Mind. Even so, within your practice, you may experience cycles of falling from and attaining enlightenment. It is important to remember that sometimes we fall from our place of wisdom specifically in order to rise up again even higher, for each time we return to the beginning, we strengthen the base of the structure that is our spiritual life.

# How Do These Broad Principles Apply to Meditation?

A student asked me how one best begins to approach God. Where does one start the spiritual journey? Any place is adequate. But the easiest place from which to begin is the point of our own perception. In other words, trust your own senses and experience. Hold fast to this beginning and everything else will follow. It's easy to become lost in sophistication and book learning. But the essence of God is very simple and graspable by all. Deuteronomy expresses this beautifully: "This teaching is not mysterious or remote from you. It is not in heaven.... It is not over the sea.... It is something very close to you. It is in your mouth and in your heart, so that you can do it."[6] The Torah says in a hundred different ways to look and see how every single aspect of nature can lead us to a sense of the divine.

The task of spirituality in general and of meditation in particular is not to make us dull or to shut us down. This is a common misconception. Rather, meditation is meant to open us up. The Jewish meditative tradition does not call for the dropping away of personality traits as, for instance, some forms of Buddhism do. Rather, each of our traits is kept and transformed. "The spark is elevated"—this is how it is usually described. The unique traits that make up each person's self are the building blocks, and we work with them rather than trying to imitate some external model.

We should enter meditation and prayer with a certain naïveté. Every one of our desires, hopes, and fears should be put into it. Rabbi Nechunia, one of the great teachers of the Talmud, was said to know all the complex kabbalistic meditations associated with prayer. But when he prayed, he would pray simply, like a small child.

Meditation can be thought of as having results that are very grandiose or very modest. I prefer that students start with rather modest ambitions. As Jonathan Omer-Man, the founder of Metivta (an acclaimed school of American Jewish meditation in Los Angeles), once said, "Meditation is boring. Don't expect more." And then he laughed. He was trying to convey a sense of proportion. We often begin a practice with the belief that enlightenment will be ours within the month. And when this fails to happen, we are bitterly disappointed. So restrained expectations are always best.

But it is also true that it is very hard to experience deep and long-term spiritual growth without incorporating into our lives some systematic contemplative practice. And meditation is the best technique we have for passing through the gateway of consciousness to the bliss of *mochin gadlut.* It offers a direct route into a greater awareness of the sweetness of existence and the curious, cranky nature of the self. Jewish meditative practice is straightforward and should not be needlessly complicated. As the Maor v'Shemesh taught, "Today it is improper to use complicated meditations—better to simply bind one's external and inner self to the *Ayn Sof...* and attach oneself to that infinite splendor."[7] However, one should always pursue this goal with a teacher; otherwise the student runs the risk of taking the wrong direction and staying mired in illusion.

To meditate, we sit quietly and become aware of each moment, each thought. During our practice it is common to become distracted. These distractions are merely white noise that moves our consciousness from the path of wisdom. Because the Jewish path embraces the notion that everything is connected and that this connection is rooted in the personal, it is understood that these distractions are not random. They have their function and should not be suppressed or even necessarily dropped away, as in a Buddhist practice. Rather, as the Baal Shem Tov taught, these thoughts enter one's mind in order that we should heal and elevate them. By noticing them and giving them over to the Holy One's purposes, we grow in intimacy with them and gain in joy, and so we arrive at healing.

Meditating in this way requires a great deal of patience. This patience with oneself and with one's practice is a very important concept to get right from the beginning. For when we can be patient with our mind's wanderings, we move closer to our own healing.

Ultimately we arrive at the perception that everything is filled with the song of God.

*Even in the inorganic things*
*such as stones or dust or water*
*there is to be found the quality*
*of soul and spiritual life.*[8]

And eventually, through many *gilgulim*, reincarnations, every soul will be received back into the One.

EXERCISE

# General Healing

When we are able to experience *chesed*, true loving-kindness, we are truly in a state of blessing and being blessed. Much of the Torah concerns itself with cultivating loving-kindness and compassion, for these are seen as being the essence of God. A simple exercise to strengthen this quality in ourselves consists of taking a phrase from the Bible that deals with *chesed* and healing and repeating it to oneself. Take fifteen minutes in the morning or evening and experiment with a few different phrases until you find one that resonates in your heart.

For example: "The one who pursues... loving-kindness finds life" (Proverbs 16:6) or "This is the kindness to show—at every place say... 'He is my brother' " (Genesis 20:13).

The next step is to fix a person in your mind's eye. You should begin, if possible, with an actual person. Try to let yourself be aware of their totality as a person, with their flaws and aches and pains. Repeat the phrase while your mind is fixed on this person. Let the phrase, with its healing energy, attach itself to the person in your consciousness.

At the end of this meditation you might feel quite fatigued. This is normal, for placing one's mind carefully and keeping the focus clear is tiring even if you have been meditating for a very long time. Be patient with yourself. As you seek to increase the *chesed* and healing of another person, inevitably it will expand to include you, the meditator, and the deepening of your own experience of *chesed* will unfold.

**CHAPTER 3**

# Understanding the Four Qualities of Consciousness

*Every day sing a new song*

*for wondrous is all of creation!*

Psalm 98

Every spiritual path requires a foundation of practice. In Hebrew, this practice is called an *avodah*. Literally this word means work, which is apt since our practice often takes on the minute-to-minute difficulty of work. But it also means service, as in service of the heart, or prayer.

We cannot assume that insight will be ours. Insight must be cultivated as one cultivates a garden or a relationship. Thus, though we start our practice from wherever we find ourselves, there are four qualities of mind that we need to cultivate. These four psychological attitudes will color all of our *avodah*, whether we are meditating, studying holy texts, washing dishes, or changing diapers. These qualities of mind are *kavannah* (passionate intentionality), *ratzon* (will), *m'sirah* (surrender), and *devekut* (attachment and rapture). This chapter takes a look at each of these attitudes.

Some months back, I was in the midst of teaching when one of my students interrupted, "But all you are saying is a matter of attitude." Most of life is a matter of attitude—a hard lesson we learned long before kindergarten. What I am saying here is not exactly that enlightenment is a matter of attitude alone. But cultivating the proper attitudes in our *avodah* is necessary if we wish our meditation to lead us to enlightenment.

Proper attitude, though wispy as smoke, can be strong as iron. Though the Jewish path is one rich in actual physical rituals, the spirit must be engaged at the same time. If mind, heart, and body are working together, the whole is strengthened, and we begin to reach our spirit's potential: enlightenment.

# *Kavannah*: The Cultivation of Passionate Intentionality

In some ways *kavannah* is similar to the Buddhist notion of mindfulness, for *kavannah*, like mindfulness, is understood to mean *attention* and *intention*. One *intends* to place one's attention on what is going on all around one. But while mindfulness in Buddhism means being aware of self or an object in a nonattached way—the emotions disentangled from the awareness—the Jewish way demands that we try to stay connected to every aspect of the ebb and flow of life. This is *hitlahavut*—the way of flame. This is why the Torah path is so committed to a communal vision of practice—to interconnected people, home, family, community, and so on.

There is a wonderful midrash that illustrates this idea of the connectedness of the physical, moral, and spiritual:

> *Rabbi Shimon said, "The Israelites are very skillful in enticing the Creator."*
>
> *Rabbi Yehuda agreed. "Yes, [they are] like expert beggars! Once one of them went to a housewife and asked for an onion. She gave it. Then he said, 'What good is an onion without bread?' so she gave him bread. The beggar then wheedled, 'You have to have something to drink if you eat dry bread!'[So she gave him something to drink—thus he received an entire meal.]"*[1]

Every aspect of this midrash portrays human beings in intimate relationship with each other and with the Infinite One. God is the housewife, feeding her clever, slightly whiny beggars. The distinction between what is mystical and what is mundane is blurred. Human beings are expected to help each other—even if they have to be nudged a bit! The Infinite is eternally influenced by the finite, and the finite is acted upon by the Infinite—in a most humorous and familial sort of way.

Through his persistence, his *kavannah*, the beggar wins from the housewife a full meal. The beggar must be sharply aware of all the dynamics going on between himself and the housewife. He must *apply* himself to getting what he needs. His attachment to the housewife is very complete. He knows what he needs, he knows what she can bestow—and he leads her along until she realizes it also. The beggar's *kavannah*, his passionate intention to get food, leads him into a relationship with the housewife, and through his persistence, both of them are changed. Our *kavannah*, our passionate intention to approach God, leads us into intimacy with the Infinite and with one another.

Here's another story that will illustrate *kavannah*. In Roptchitz, where the *tzaddik* Naftali lived (a *tzaddik* is a fully enlightened being), it was the custom for rich people whose houses stood isolated to hire men to watch over their property by night. Late one evening Naftali was skirting the woods that surrounded the city and meditating on the moon when he encountered a watchman.

"For whom are you working?" the *tzaddik* asked.

Not recognizing him, the watchman inquired in turn, "For whom are you working, Rebbe?"

The words struck the *tzaddik* like an arrow. "I am not working for anybody just yet," he whispered and began walking back and forth in great agitation and whispering to himself, "For whom am I working, for whom am I working?" Finally he stopped and turned to the watchman. "Will you come and work for me?" he asked.

The watchman asked, "But what would be my duties?"

"To remind me," murmured the *tzaddik*.

This story illustrates the land of attention necessary for our practice. The *tzaddik*, already enlightened, recognizes that his attention could be even more sharply focused.

A final anecdote about *kavannah*. For many years I made my living as a roofer and shingler. My job was to lay out cedar shingles in proper patterns on the roof and then drive the nails. It was a job that was conducive, once I got used to it, to a certain detachment and daydreaming. Because it was repetitious (once the shingles were aligned, it was only a matter of keeping everything straight while I nailed them down), the mind could wander, think great thoughts, and go off on great meditations. But I noticed that no matter how spiritual and "high" I got, if I misplaced my attention and hit my thumb with the hammer, all my senses and concentration suddenly came back to that one square inch of my body. And the holy thoughts? Nowhere to be found. Or at least they didn't make my thumb feel any better. But I did feel a great deal of passion in those moments! *Kavannah* is to place our attention on what we are doing; then, by being in the moment, we experience joy in the doing.

Jewish spirituality suggests that we bring awareness to all of our actions (which we call *mitzvot*). Our *kavannah*, our passionate intent, brings us into deeper contact with all of life, even the painful parts. For if we wall ourselves off from life because we believe that life is suffering and filled with pain, we will end up walling ourselves away from the joy and infinite sweetness of existence, and we will thus barricade the direct road to wisdom and enlightenment.

# *Ratzon*: The Cultivation of Passionate Will

We *will* ourselves to begin and continue a practice. When we are motivated to begin a spiritual practice, *ratzon* is that gritty part of us that makes us go sign up for a class or makes us meditate even when we feel fatigued. It is pure stubbornness. This is a quality that cannot be underestimated in terms of its importance for a successful *avodah*.

*Ratzon* is also, however, a quality that can easily get out of hand. It belongs to the family of qualities that derive from *gevurah*—strictness, control, harshness, and strength. *Ratzon*, a will that is passionate, is of fundamental importance, but it can easily begin to control the student rather than the student controlling it. Most of the complaints one hears about

Judaism come from a misunderstanding of this quality or from this aspect of mind getting out of control. This is the quality behind harsh zealotry. As Pinchas Shapiro of Kuretz, a Chasidic master, once said, "Woe to the generation when the zealots come together!"[2]

To have a strong spiritual practice, we must fill our day with physical actions, including rituals, that are consistent and strong. All these *mitzvot* are designed to lead us to enlightenment, which is a surrender to the Infinite. Moses Maimonides, the great Jewish philosopher, wrote at the end of his book *Hilchot T'murah* that "most laws of Torah are suggestions from a distant past ... to improve our perception and make us straight."[3] We must utilize our *ratzon*, our will, to truly implement the suggestions of the Torah. But the passage from strong to strict can be very smooth and quick. And the movement from strictness to humorless fanaticism is just as smooth. Be strict, but don't be too strict. Too much strictness is the advice of demons. Practice diligently, with a passionate will, but keep a sense of humor. The growth of *chesed* (of which humor is a part) will be one of the most sustaining and important parts of your practice. Once this is lost (and it is easily lost), *ratzon* can run amok.

For example, sometimes a student who has recently begun a practice will find it becoming very easy and uplifting. She will experience a kind of "runner's high"—so much so that she may begin to think that she's not doing enough. This easily translates into a feeling of failure. So the student becomes more and more strict in ritual observance and takes on many more *mitzvot.*

Left unchecked, this fear of failure or sense of not doing enough will lead the student to depression, which is exactly the opposite of the state of mind desired. Our *avodah* is cumulative, and except in rare cases, it is gradual. The student should confer closely with his or her teacher on this matter, but generally speaking, simple persistence (deriving from *ratzon)* will eventually bring the student to the state of *mochin gadlut*, Great Mind.

On the other hand, you must not fool yourself and allow yourself to be lazy. Your *avodah* is intended to move you from a state of sleep to a state of wakefulness, from a state of looking through a fog to being able to see with great clarity. *Ratzon* is one of the keys to this.

Harness *ratzon* so that it spurs you first to a greater *kavannah* (intention) of effort, and then, when your effort has proved successful and you begin to taste the joy provided by insight and wisdom, continue to harness it for the greater clarity that comes with union with the Infinite.

Just do it; put your money where your mouth is—all the clichés are true. To attain the nectar of the Infinite, one must use *ratzon*, for ultimately it alone has the power to move us forward in our practice. Using it fully but without fanaticism is vital for anyone on a spiritual journey. Though *ratzon* can be, if not properly held in check, coercive and burdensome, it is nonetheless an irreplaceable component of a meditative life.

# *M'sirah*: The Cultivation of Surrender

When I first became a father, I thought my life would remain essentially unchanged. I figured I would play with the children and help change their diapers and so on, but the essential me and the rest of my life would go on pretty much the same.

This naive vision was soon readjusted. Babies need absolutely constant attention (*kavannah*); to give this attention properly, one must surrender to their need. For example, if the baby has colic or stomach flu and is up all night for several nights, crying in pain and vomiting or having diarrhea (or both), you must switch over to a no-sleep mode. You cannot punish the baby (God forbid!) for something like this. The baby is unaware of your need, and this is as it should be. The baby is a new, very innocent soul placed in your hands to nurture. You cannot explain that you need to rest. All you can do is … surrender.

But the moment you do surrender to her need, you begin to receive a great payment in return. This awareness comes and goes, of course, depending on the state of your surrender, but the idea is plain. The cliché is perfectly true and eminently Jewish—that by giving love we receive it back a hundredfold. This is one of the prime meanings of the Mishnah when it urges, "Be like a servant who serves without thought of reward." In other words, surrender to the service and to love itself. Giving love even past the point where it is easy helps us break through a particular barrier of self. One should try to practice this in as many situations as possible—surrendering to a loved one, to a specific bit of work, to our general position in the world. The Jewish path does not advocate mindless acceptance of pain or suffering; oppression in and of itself does not annihilate the ego. On the other hand, the line between ego and proper respect for self can be very easily blurred, and there is a way in which the ego must shrink in order for the heart to expand so that God can enter.

It is difficult indeed to bring our consciousness consistently to *m'sirah*, to the surrender of self into the *Ayn Sof*. This may well be the most difficult part of our entire *avodah*. But it is of utmost importance. For it not only opens the channels of self to greater insight into the unity of creation, but it is also a self-reinforcing strategy. In other words, the more you practice surrender to the flow of love that permeates creation, the more your *kavannah* will grow and the stronger you will become in your *avodah*.

We often tend to translate surrender as adjusting. There is a goal—let us call it "enlightenment"—and the path to that goal seems to require a certain discipline or series of practices. So we adjust our internal clock, our internal discipline factor, to be able to handle this extra work. But really, in our hearts, we are simply doing an unpleasant duty. This is the attitude inside many synagogues and churches. We go, but as a matter of obligation alone. True surrender, on the other hand, is a purely internal thing. We do a practice in order to cultivate the spirit of *m'sirah*—so that surrender flows more easily. Thus, we may fulfill an obligation in order for surrender to occur—but surrender and obligation are not the same thing. Surrender is not the same as simply adjusting to a situation. When we surrender, we are not diminished. What falls away is ego, leaving us, ultimately, enhanced. Just as when we fall in love, we fall away from the place of ego.

A famous story illustrates this point: Rebbe Leib went to study with the Mezritcher rebbe. "Why are you going?" his friends asked. "You are a great Torah scholar. You certainly know as much if not more Torah than the Mezritcher."

"Oh, I am not going to learn Torah," Rebbe Leib said. "I am going to watch him tie and untie his shoelaces."

Leib realized that achieving union with God was not a matter of learning alone. There was another level, and to get to that level he needed to surrender his vaunted position as a Torah scholar. He needed to watch the Mezritcher tie his shoelaces. Foolish? Of course foolish! In one sense we are all fools: We go on struggling, even though we know we can't get out of the world alive; we get ourselves into impossible situations and then cry about it. We are all beloved, foolish children of God. Leib was not worried about being a fool. He wanted to break through to the place where tying and untying his shoelaces were also acts of holiness.

There is a story about the great *tzaddik* Simcha Bunam. When he was dying, his disciples and family gathered around his bed. They were very upset and began weeping and carrying on. Bunam pulled himself up in bed with a roar and shouted, "Why are you all so upset? My whole life was just a preparation for learning how to die!"

Surrender demands that we perceive that everything is changeable and ongoing. As Koheleth taught:

*To everything there is a season*
*and there is a time to every purpose under heaven.*
*A time to be born and a time to die—*

*A time to plant and a time to uproot—*
*A time to kill and a time to heal— ...*
*A time to love and a time to hate—*
*A time of war and a time of peace.*[4]

*M'sirah*, surrender, means finally accepting death. Nothing that exists goes on forever. No superego survives death. No river stands in the same place for very long—it flows on and on. Because we try to hold on to things, because we try to hold out against death, we become afraid of life. But death and life are part of the same process. And surrender is a type of death. This is what makes it so hard! Surrender is the death of ego, the giving over of ego to the *Ayn Sof.* In the deepest sense, this is an aspect of love, which is why many people are afraid of it. When we are truly in love, we surrender a part of our ego. We give over ourselves to our lover, our child, our parent, our friend, our spouse.

True life can only begin with the surrender of the ego. The soul, after all, is egoless. Surrender means letting go of all the preconceptions, all the accumulations of life, which is always temporary and changing. Listen to this story:

Once a tourist was buying souvenirs near Mount Vernon. He picked up an ancient ax in an antique store. "That there is the genuine ax George Washington used to cut down the cherry tree," the store owner proudly proclaimed.

"Really?" the tourist exclaimed. "It doesn't look *that* old."

"Well," the shopkeeper admitted, "it has had two new handles and three new heads."

Every bit of life goes on exchanging heads and handles. To recognize this is to surrender to the flux of existence. Once we surrender, then we fully recognize that there is something beyond life and death. This is the *Ayn Sof* itself. All of life is just a short loop on a track that takes us back to the original source from which we came. It is, so to speak, a training ground only. The moment you surrender, you disappear. The moment you disappear, God appears. There is no greater joy than this. Ramakrishna, a mad, God-intoxicated Indian, described, in a way that has always touched me, how we can recognize this: "My dear friend, when you hear one of the glorious Divine Names—be it Allah, Tara, Krishna ... if tears of ecstasy come spontaneously to your eyes ... this is authentic confirmation that you are awakening."[5]

# *Devekut*: The Cultivation of Rapturous Union

*Devekut* is usually translated as "attachment." But this quality of mind actually comes when the attachment has been accomplished and the flow between the soul and the Infinite One runs free. *Sefer Haredim*, a sixteenth-century book of spiritual teachings, defines *devekut* as "the most passionate love, [when] you are not separated from the [Infinite One] for even a moment."[6]

Many traditions seek to lessen our attachment to the world. This is especially true in Buddhism and ascetic forms of Christianity. Buddhism considers attachment to the senses, to objects, and to the passions of the world as being profoundly counterproductive to the pursuit of wisdom or enlightenment. And though there are many examples in Judaism that also reflect a profound distrust of worldly attachment, it seems to me that the Jewish way views the senses, the passions, and all of creation as being passionately joined. All of these feelings and states are methods by which union with the divine Infinite can be achieved. The Baal Shem Tov used to quote a psalm to illustrate this: "In all of your ways know Him"—that is, with our tears, our laughter, our passion, our mind, and with all the manifold gifts of life and nature. In the Jewish tradition we seek attachment to the Infinite, not detachment. "[When] you connect with even one *mitzvah* ... with love ... you grasp part of the Unity [for each part is connected to the whole]."[7] Torah reflects a view of the universe in which all things are attached to one another in an intimate, close, personal way.

The first stage of *devekut* is accepting the *possibility* that passionate union with the Infinite can in fact happen and that we are worthy of *chokhmat lev*, wisdom of the heart. This stage involves accepting the possibility that there may be something to this spirituality business after all. The first step in experiencing *devekut* is admitting this "may be," this "could be" into our consciousness.

Once the Berditchever rebbe was going to visit a town famous for its atheism and lack of spirituality, One of the teachers of the town came to him, determined to debate him and blast apart his arguments. The rebbe had just finished his prayers. As he walked on, he looked at the young teacher with tears in his eyes and said, "But perhaps it [God—and all that this assumes] is, after all." These simple words struck the young man like a thunderbolt and forced him to reexamine himself. Of course, the story goes on to say that this young man became a famous rebbe in his own right.

*Devekut* is the actual experience of the bliss of the *Ayn Sof*, the Without-End. So intense can be the pleasure gleaned from this attachment that it has been described in the most effusive and romantic ways imaginable. For instance:

> *A person whose consciousness is always attached [to the* Ayn Sof] *... enjoys great delight at every moment, for the root of soul is attached.... If he were to stop serving for even a moment he would immediately feel the absence of this great pleasure. Knowing that, he will make sure not to separate himself from ... service for even the briefest moment, so as not to be exposed to the harshness of that deprivation.*[8]

How is *devekut* a cultivation of mind? The mind is like a field. We seed it and hope for growth. If we want to continue working this field, we must experience some harvest or we will not try to seed it again. Just so, in cultivating the mind, we need to experience some *devekut*, some harvest of rapturous connection, in order to move toward full *devekut*. In the Jewish tradition, we are taught that in fact almost all of us *have* felt this connection at various moments and in various places. It may not necessarily have been a "religious" moment. The experience of rapturous attachment can come while taking a bath, playing with our children, or driving to work in rush-hour traffic (though I personally think this must be rare). To recall, to permit, to experience passionate connection—this is *devekut*. It is the mystery of the kiss in the Song of Songs, where all the greatest mysteries of Torah and enlightenment are described as being given over with a kiss. It is not the description of the kiss but the kiss itself. One of my teachers used to say, "You know, when you kiss someone, you don't say a word…. [It] must be the kiss itself."[9]

We can elaborate on this metaphor of passion to illustrate the difference between *kavannah* and *devekut*. *Devekut* is the fruit of the endeavor. If *kavannah* is viewed as the desire, then *devekut* is the orgasm. *Devekut* is the union itself, the union maximized. And though we do not make love just for the sake of the orgasm, yet in fact, that point of transcendent pleasure is one of the true motivators, one of the cultivations of mind necessary for the discipline to continue. We do not grow a fruit tree *only* for the fruit, but if the fruit tree never yields fruit, we will in time cut it down and replace it with another.

So, these are the stages in cultivating *devekut*: First, we must accept the possibility that rapture is possible. (This is often the most difficult step.) Then we must keep ourselves always ready to receive the divine *shefa*, flow, of ecstasy. Finally, we come to accept all of life with joy and an open heart, permitting it to consume us—and letting it go without rancor when it departs.

There is no easy way to sum up these four qualities of mind. At times they work consecutively, and at times emphasis is placed on one. A simple self-awareness that these are states of mind that *can be cultivated* is an important tool for spiritual growth. During the course of a day we will draw upon an awareness of all these states. For example, one might wake up in the morning feeling drained of all energy. Even to blink seems impossible! The best thing to do is place our awareness on *ratzon*, will, and use that quality of mind to get us out of bed and begin the day's practice. Of course a diet of *ratzon* alone is very dry fare, so as quickly as we can, we try to engage our *kavannah*. Perhaps we listen to a piece of music. Concentrating on it, we let our mood lighten and the awareness of our inner potential grow. By *letting* our mood lighten, we have begun to engage *m'sirah*, surrender, which will ease the difficulty of engaging *ratzon*, will intensify our *kavannah*, and eventually will lead us back to inner transformation—that is, *devekut*, which is union itself.

There is no proper order to these mind states. The context and situation of the moment will dictate which inner response is called for.

## EXERCISE

# Cultivation of Surrender and Will

This is an exercise that will help to cultivate both the qualities of *m'sirah* and *ratzon*. It incorporates a traditional aspect of an *avodah*, which is the process of scrutinizing oneself and making what is called a *cheshbon nefesh*, a soul accounting.

Set for yourself a certain period of time— say, three weeks. Every evening, either while you are sitting in meditation or while you are lying in bed, spend a few minutes contemplating the day's activities. Bring to mind the various times you were angry, short-tempered, slipped into depression, and lost the place of joy. Do not permit extra guilt feelings to arise from these recollections; simply see them in the mind's eye. Psychically gather them together and offer them in your prayer or meditation as a *korban,* a sacrifice. Say this prayer: "These angers and fears, Lord, they are yours. Take them as a sacrifice. All of the negative thoughts and feelings I had today, I offer over to you as a gift of my mortality. Lord of the Infinite, please transform them into love."

The act of taking some of our anger and fear and offering them over as a *korban* often requires a tremendous amount of will. This exercise will strengthen this quality of soul precisely because it is difficult to manage.

In doing this exercise certain questions and difficulties may arise. Besides the obvious difficulty of continuing with the exercise because of boredom or distraction, additional problems that might surface have to do with deep-seated emotional memories. For many people, any surrender meditation has the problem of loss or lack of control. This feeling often surfaces during this meditation with startling swiftness. If you encounter this problem, treat yourself like a beginning swimmer. You don't want to go too deep too fast. Go a little way, then return. The next time, go a little deeper. As you become more familiar with the meditation, greater degrees of release will occur. The release is often experienced as euphoria or vast relief. Such feelings are splendid but will evaporate in time, leaving you, the meditator, the option of going ever deeper in your soul work.

# CHAPTER 4

# Recognizing Obstacles

*When you want to enter the higher*

*worlds ...* klippot *[obstacles] will*

*stand in your way. ... Continue*

*to work with all your might, and*

*in the end you will ... enter*

*the higher worlds.*

The Baal Shem Tov,

from *Sefer Baal Shem Tov*

Bereshit

A spiritual practice is meant to lead to greater insight and joy. But the path to this state can often be rocky. The pains that arise are inevitable. Ideally they should be embraced as part of the process of understanding. But this is asking a lot. I will give you the advice that I give my students: Try to reflect, in some corner of your mind, that the difficulties that surface in your life may be avenues toward greater understanding, no matter how improbable this seems at the time. To accept this is the work of a lifetime, but one can begin by accepting the *possibility* that such is the case.

In Hebrew, all hindrances, regardless of their shape and size, are called *klippot (klippah* is the singular version). Literally meaning shells or husks, this term refers to their nature as barriers. They block the light of infinite vision with the shell of their illusion. Of course this shell is very strong. If it were not, it could not hinder us so thoroughly.

There are many general kinds of *klippot* as well as specific and general strategies for dealing with them. But the best way is with humor and patience. It is said that the active force of the *klippot*—what we may call the Trickster, the contrary impulse, the Satan, or the Adversary—is actually a *helpful* angel. Its purpose is to draw us out, to confront us and help us bloom. There is a famous midrash that illustrates this: There is not a blade of grass that grows without its own private angel standing behind, striking it with an iron bar, saying, Grow! Grow!

It is an awkward fact that sometimes we learn from a kiss and sometimes from a blow, sometimes from leniency and sometimes from harshness. The *klippah* applies pressure that we must push against in order to grow. Indeed, the angel of a *klippah* is said to utter a blessing of joy every time a person overcomes him. There is often a *klippah* around our consciousness. When we are hindered or hurt, this *klippah* exerts pressure on us to stop perceiving and to react only in anger. If the pressure from this *klippah* can be overcome, then commensurate strength and insight are generated. But our response to the *klippah* must be genuine. Fake smiles are almost as bad as anger.

Several primary *klippot* are defined in Jewish practice, and they are approached in different ways. In this chapter, we will deal briefly with the *klippot* of pride, distraction, doubt, and guilt. We may think of these as the four foundation obstacles. One way or another, to make spiritual progress, we must deal with these four.

But first, a word of caution. We all suffer from the obstacles and pains of life. And the Jewish tradition lists several strategies for dealing with these. But the deepest truth is that all things come from God and all that God gives is good. This is called a mystery, meaning that it is a truth very difficult to experience in the heart. The words can be said easily, but the *inner truth* of it—this is very difficult. One person's suffering may be another person's good fortune. But it goes even deeper than this. Everything that happens is part of God, so really there are no obstacles; there is only the One. But *saying* this and *knowing* this are very different things. Hence, we approach this understanding slowly, through examining the *klippot* and learning to deal with them one at a time. Let's begin with a story that illustrates the Jewish understanding that everything, even suffering, is one within God:

Disciples once came to the Mezritcher *tzaddik.* "We have read in scripture that we should praise and thank God for suffering just as for well-being and receive it with the same joy. How can we understand this?"

He replied, "Go to the house of study and ask for Reb Zusya. He is a man who from the day of his birth has experienced great privation."

They went and found Reb Zusya. They said, "The *tzaddik* told us that you would explain how to praise and thank God for the suffering that befalls us."

"There must be some mistake," Reb Zusya laughed. "By God's mercy I have received only bounty and blessing all my life!"

Zusya, you see, realized that everything comes from the good. He knew this not just in his mind but in his heart. At the same time, this is almost a cliché, something almost every teacher tells us. What practical good is it? Few are the individuals who can remember this advice when evil descends on them. Zusya, however, had completely broken through. He knew that the distinction between good and evil is an illusion —it is all good! All from God!

Most of us need an intermediate step in order to grasp this. The Talmud calls this intermediate concept *gam zeh l'tovah*, meaning "this also is for the best." Another story makes this point: Once there was a little tailor who was told his son had badly fractured his leg. The bearers of the news lamented, "Poor little tailor, to suffer such misfortune." But the tailor shrugged and replied, "Maybe not." The next day all the young men were drafted to fight in the czar's army except his son, exempted because of his leg.

As long as we are in the body, we are vulnerable to pain. It is unavoidable. A spiritual practice (and meditation most especially) helps to slow us down so we may grasp the nature of our own internal response to what is happening. Even more, such practice brings us tools for understanding our deepest selves. Similarly, a clear understanding of the *klippot* helps us to overcome the obstacles to our practice.

# The *Klippah* of Pride

The nature of will and the nature of ego are very close. A person who has labored long with his or her spiritual discipline often has great pride. These are the people who have been punctilious about the law, observed the fasts, and given much time and energy to meditation and prayer. But this work and devotion have a hidden danger, which is the danger of pride. Pride is not the same as enjoying the labor or even rejoicing in one's accomplishment. These two feelings rest on the knowledge that life is temporary. Pride, on the other hand, knows of no future other than itself. Filled with itself, it believes that all reality revolves around it.

The following story describes the danger that pride can bring to our practice: Naftali the *tzaddik* was sitting at home one evening and heard a knock at the door. He answered. Standing there was a young man dressed in the robes of a scholar.

"Rebbe," he said, "I have come to study with you."

"Really?" said the rebbe. "What have you learned so far in your studies?"

"A tremendous amount," said the young man. "I have memorized all of Torah and most of Talmud."

"I am sorry, young man, I cannot teach you," the *tzaddik* said and closed the door.

A little later there was another knock. He answered it, and a young woman was there. "Excuse me, Rebbe," she said. "I would like to learn with you."

"And what have you learned of Torah up to now?" he asked sternly.

"To tell you the truth, I know nothing," she said.

"Come in, come in," he said, smiling broadly.

Later his wife asked him the meaning of this strange behavior. "The first lesson and the most important—the one we must always begin with every year, every day, every moment—is that we know nothing. If we come from a place of thinking we know, it is very hard to progress."

The *klippah* of pride is very easy to fall into. Indeed, it is the most difficult obstacle to avoid. Sometimes when I am teaching, someone in the audience will ask a question and I will grow impatient, thinking, "That's not the right question to ask! They haven't understood what I was talking about at all!" Ha! It is my own craziness, thinking that I know the right question a person should ask!

We can easily transform the spiritual into something base. We can take emotion or thought and lower it to a place of pride. That is, we may have a true experience of joy in accomplishment and in the next moment debase it into a feeling of superiority over other people. But "pride goes before a fall," as the proverb aptly puts it. When we enter into a place of pride, even of spiritual pride, we quickly fall from whatever real attainment we have achieved.

I have heard a story: There was once a rabbi *davvening*, praying, Yom Kippur. He stood before the Holy Ark and cried out, "Master of the universe! I am nothing!" A few minutes later the cantor stepped out, spread his arms wide, and cried out with an equally loud voice, "Master of the world! I am nothing!" Carried away by all this spiritual energy, Moshe the shoemaker stepped up also and cried out, "Master of the universe! I am nothing!"

The rabbi, who was standing on the podium, nudged the cantor and whispered to him, "Oy vey, look who thinks he's nothing."

It's very easy to be entranced with the notion of our own great attainment. This problem is especially true for teachers, but it is something that every practitioner must watch out for. "Oy vey, look who thinks he's nothing." As the Baal Shem Tov taught, we can be totally enlightened one minute and completely fallen from that high rung the next. Some of our teachers of blessed memory taught that "[some] people are sent into the world only for the purpose of figuring out how to avoid the pitfall of pride."[1]

One of the ways in which I pay for my mortgage and health insurance is by teaching children Jewish spirituality. I recommend this as an antidote for every person who works in a spiritual vein. It's very hard to wobble off course when one is trying to give spiritual lessons to kids. If you become distracted or puffed up, the kids are onto it in a minute and will call down thunder and lightning with their laughter or snores. True focus is taught not by me to the kids but by the kids to me. Every abstraction must be thought through until it hits something concrete. Every highfalutin phrase is exposed to the harsh reality of children's good-natured but searing consciousness. Children are good teachers; I recommend them with all my heart.

Of course pride is an aspect of ego. It comes and goes in a moment. But while it is affecting us it is very powerful. We can fight it by cultivating the four positive mind states of *kavannah, m'sirah, ratzon,* and *devekut.* In overcoming pride, we learn humility, one of the cardinal virtues. Without humility we cannot drop any measure of ego; our pride gets in the way. Pride is a part of ego. It is a piece of personality that is an obstacle to greater spiritual growth. It is not an innate part of the soul. It can be dropped, with steady *avodah,* practice.

# The *Klippah* of Distraction

In a spiritual practice generally (but especially in meditation), extraneous thoughts and distractions are a perennial problem. The sufis call the mind the wild horse that wanders far and wide. Whatever there is to think about, the mind will inevitably seize on it. Most traditions advocate either suppressing these distracting thoughts or letting them drift away. Some advocate a nonattached examination; then let them glide by. It is reflective of the rather intimate Jewish attitude to spirituality that most Jewish teachers advocate something slightly different regarding these disturbances. Though a generally nonattached awareness is a good starting point for dealing with distractions, a deeper level of awareness can be reached by bringing the distractions into consciousness so they can serve the ongoing *avodah,* practice, of the meditator.

In the last chapter we touched on the practice of elevating our thoughts. This practice is an especially helpful way of dealing with distracting thoughts during meditation. By elevating the thought—that is, by recognizing that it, too, is part of the Infinite One and by giving it over to God's purposes—we use it to draw closer to God. As one early teacher said, "When an extraneous thought comes to you … you can use that thought itself to bind yourself to God all the more."[2]

Distractions of everyday life can also get in the way of our spiritual growth. Being busy is a great *klippah* of distraction; it can prevent us from sitting down to meditate in the first place. It is to this distracting *klippah* that the Torah addresses itself when it describes the meeting of God and Moses. It says that God speaks to Moses from a thick, impenetrable cloud. But why from behind such a shield? It is because there are times when we must silence ourselves completely in order to hear God. We must enter a space where there is no distraction from the world around us. Although we will always return to the world, there are times when we must withdraw. This is the necessary silence of the cloud. And this is the silence that the *klippah* of distraction will try to prevent us from reaching.

Still, every attempt to calm the mind will initially be met with a playful and confused response. The mind will leap about. All of the meditation techniques used in all of the religions are geared to directing energy, laserlike, in the right direction. Prayer, chant, song, silent meditation—it makes no difference. One of their purposes is always to quiet and direct the mind.

But we must always come back to the realization that distractions have their purpose and place. Sometimes distractions are placed in the stream of the mind by the intimacy that connects the world. They are not useless. In meditation, as in prayer and in our daily life, we need to dedicate these distractions to our greater understanding. Every distraction is a potential doorway to deeper enlightenment.

# The *Klippah* of Doubt

Faith and doubt are mirror images of each other. They stand looking into each other's eyes. You cannot have one without the other. I have heard that there was once a town that had no rain for five years. The people were desperate. They decided to get together and pray for rain. They would wail and scream, hoping this would soften the heart of heaven. Pulling out all the stops, they would throw themselves on the mercy of God.

The whole town went out to the meadow to begin. Suddenly there was a roar of laughter from the back of the crowd. Everyone looked down and saw a small child carrying an umbrella! "What is this you are doing, little one? Why are you carrying an umbrella? You might lose it. It's not raining."

The child replied, "But I thought when you prayed the rains would come."

This is faith, and in the statement of the adults is its shadow, doubt. If everyone in the town had had faith that the rains would come—ah, the rain would still be pouring!

Sometimes doubt will manifest itself through simple boredom. The meditation is flat. The songs are repetitious. One's teacher is mundane. One's community is banal. One simply becomes weary of the whole thing. Enough!

This type of withdrawal is insidious. One step of withdrawal leads to the next until we are very far from God's presence. When one is seeking to ignite the heart, there are often many false flare-ups and flickerings. Like lighting a campfire, you may have to make many attempts before you have a steadily burning flame.

Often doubt will create in us an inordinate desire to be "authentic." This kind of doubt pushes us to find the "real" spirituality, and we find ourselves desperately holding on to the most reactionary traditionalism. But what is authentic in a spiritual sense is simply what works. Our teachers of blessed memory have passed on to us their "authentic" tradition—that is, the techniques and ideology that worked for them. It is our duty to use this tradition, tinker with it, build on it, but never to mistake it for the authentic experience itself, which is the experience of God.

All of us want to do it "right" and to be "honest," both during meditation and in general. But one of the splendid ironies of the spiritual path is that "rightness" is very slippery, much dependent on the eye of the beholder. The desire to be authentic is good, but it can also cause the student's consciousness to start turning round and round, examining and reexamining itself until he is half crazy. Such an ongoing self-examination will often cause the student to lose sight of his chief aid in penetrating the play of illusion (*gashmiyut*). Students may become suspicious of their attachment to joy and love. In pushing to "further" their insight, they may become dour, depressed, and pained. In short, they may become people who do not give much pleasure to themselves and are certainly not much fun to be around. In the *Tzavat Rivash*, the Baal Shem Tov advises students "not to be too strict in any practice. Too much strictness makes us think … we haven't done things exactly right and [we] become depressed. Depression is the single greatest barrier to experiencing God."[3] By using *ratzon* and *devekut*, we can move from doubt and depression toward belief.

In the morning service, there are the lines *"Ani maamin h'emunah sh'lemah,"* "I believe with perfect faith." The Chasidic tradition points out that no one has perfect faith. Doubt intrudes whether we wish it or not. So how can we say that we believe with perfect faith, knowing we lie? The answer comes: Even though we doubt, we seek to move ourselves in the direction of belief.

# The *Klippah* of Guilt

Guilt is a zealot. It is alone and unforgiving. When we feel guilty or direct blame either back toward ourselves or outward to others, we are failing to recognize the fluid, wavering nature of reality. Instead, we are seeking to nail down verities, which do not in fact exist. There is a well-known teaching in Chasidism that *"ayn to'kokah b'dor hazeh,"* "there is no rebuking in this generation." Because how can one rebuke when there is no true knowledge of motive or outcome? A great master (the Ishbitzer *tzaddik)* wrote that in the fullness of time "God will make it clear [there] is only good, and sin is only in … the mind [insignificant as] a garlic husk."[4]

The Jewish tradition often speaks of the uniqueness of each person and the miracle of each person's consciousness. Clearly a life is not something to be squandered. Guilt and blame are *klippot* that squander time. They are essentially frozen moments, lacking vitality. They hold the mind in a place of *klippah.* Until one can step away from blaming oneself or blaming others, progress cannot be made.

Many Jews complain that they were brought up to believe Judaism is a path of guilt. It is true there is a lot of guilt among Jews. Paradoxically, this guilt stems from the personal and intimate nature of the Jewish path. No one can push our buttons more easily than other family members! It is intimacy itself that permits family to get under our skin. Judaism is the path of intimacy. Blame and guilt are dangers that arise when we are intimate.

There is no question that guilt is a powerful tool; it can motivate one to act in situations where action is required—for instance, in working for social justice. But as a tool of spiritual advancement it is very limited. You cannot get to a place of spiritual expansiveness through a method of constriction. The dangers inherent in guilt are profound and difficult to avoid. It can paralyze us. It clouds the mind and keeps us from moving forward in wisdom. Guilt almost inevitably leads to depression, and depression can be an implacable hindrance in the Jewish path.

The Baal Shem Tov once commented that people who make a mistake or commit a transgression often feel guilty, and this guilt makes them feel awful. "Now," he exclaimed, "they have done two sins. And then they will feel guilty about feeling guilty! Three sins! Where does it stop?"

Where to stop it is right here, wherever you are. We usually know the general direction we need to follow for our spiritual well-being and growth. The effort lies in turning ourselves in that direction. Blame and guilt are made-up walls that block the path.

By dropping false guilt, guilt that arises and paralyzes us, we begin to enter a very spacious place of mind. The feeling is one of great freedom, lightness, and joy. It is the very stuff of *mochin gadlut*, enlightenment. When we can let go of guilt we immediately have entry into our true nature, which is godly.

# Light for the Darkness

The Jewish path is very much against the idea that one can uproot or cut out *any* character trait. What we have, we have. To try to destroy any of these qualities is the same as trying to destroy a piece of the soul. Even the most negative character traits, such as jealousy and hatred, cannot be tortured out of our consciousness. Standing in the dark, a person may become angry with the dark and begin shouting, "Out, get out!" and swinging a stick to make it leave. But the stick will not dispel the darkness, nor will it bring the light no matter how long or vigorously she swings it. Only a little light can dispel darkness. What is needed is not to suppress our negative qualities but to gain greater access to our positive qualities. There is a verse in Psalms that says "avoid evil and do good." Some Chasidim ask, how can one avoid evil? The answer is there: by doing good.

Doing good means that we try to manifest the mental and spiritual gains made in meditation. It means being compassionate when you don't initially feel like it. It means catching yourself before you are rude to the waitress or angry at your children—and trying to turn your thought to one of friendliness and peacefulness, It means to actively give *tzedakah*, charity, and help your neighbor. It means practicing what you preach.

By advising us to bring light to the darkness, I am not advocating denial of the darkness. The Torah path is meant to put us in touch with the infinite love of God, but it is not meant to make us liars or hypocrites. When there is pain, there is pain. It does no good to deny its reality or even to tell ourselves it is all part of God's plan when we don't really believe it—even when it is. A person can be depressed—and often we have a right to be depressed. There is a joke that goes like this: This world is in need of so much healing, if a person is well adjusted, he must be crazy! In dire circumstances it is nearly impossible to to feel God's benevolent presence. To pretend that everything is good in such situations only leads to hypocrisy and does not serve our best spiritual interests. When deep pain and wounding occur, it is best to feel their totality—but let yourself come out on the other side and be healed.

Life is sometimes hard. But pride, distraction, doubt, and guilt lead us ever further from the goal, which is an opening of the mind to the Infinite. Yet overcoming these obstacles can be our greatest opportunity to practice the four qualities of consciousness, *kavannah* (intent), *ratzon* (will), *m'sirah* (surrender), and *devekut* (rapturous union), leavened with a liberal dose of humor and patience, are the foundation of spiritual practice. The Torah path wants to teach us that life is an unfolding. It calls not for a denial of pain but for an acceptance of the possibility of joy.

EXERCISE

# Overcoming Doubt

*Klippot* are the shadow side of discipline and attainment. There are many exercises that serve to dispel them during meditation. It is ideal to have a teacher you trust in this phase of learning and practice. Here is an exercise to help you deal with the *klippah* of doubt.

When you meditate, try to put yourself physically in a place that normally gives you happiness. For starters, this may simply mean sitting in a chair and putting on some music you like. Sit quietly for fifteen minutes, watching your thoughts. Notice the doubts that arise during meditation. These might be: Why am I doing this when I could be at a movie? It might be a statement that arises in the mind such as: This is boring! When one of these thoughts crops up, first reassure yourself that your will can overcome this doubt. Then stop to examine the doubt itself. Become familiar with it. From where does it arise? Is the doubt arising simply because you're bored? Restless? How important, really, is the doubt that arises? Remember, what you are endeavoring to do here is gain control of the mind. Few things are as important as this. Breathe deeply and allow yourself to stay calm and centered while you do this. Remember that your ability to recognize such obstacles is the first and most important step to overcoming them.

Next, call to mind the beauty of a well-loved natural setting or the face of a loved one. Concentrate on how this recollection fills you with happiness. Slowly expand this picture, including more and more friends, more and more aspects of inspiring nature. Now reflect on the strength you have when hindrances are not pulling you down. Let the picture of beauty pull you *up* rather than letting the hindrances pull you *down*. Let yourself remember that purpose and joy will result in achievement. Knowing this is not vanity, but true vision. You will feel the victory of joy over despair. Practice this meditation every day for a month, and you will experience a qualitative shift in your consciousness. This meditation can be used to great advantage every time doubts begin to surface in the mind.

**CHAPTER 5**

# Setting Up Your Own Practice

*God does not derive great delight*

*from us when we blend ourselves*

*together.... [Rather] God desires*

*our detailed individuality, each*

*within our separate body—this is*

*what gives him great delight.*

Zev Wolf of Zhitomir

Setting up our own practice is at once simple and difficult. There is no single right way to do it. No one model will work for all of us, for we all go about our practice differently and begin with different strengths and weaknesses. The return on such effort is very great, but the initial exacting nature of the work can also be very frustrating. It may help for the reader to know some of my own failures, successes, and ongoing struggles in this regard, so I have included my story at the end of the chapter.

But the first thing we must start with is of course ourselves. We must engage ourselves in our practice. This chapter describes several different ways in which we can attach ourselves and continue to be attached to our *avodah*. For example, entering into community is a time-honored Jewish way of engaging in spiritual practice, as is the broad category of *tikkun*, or healing. But what then? How, practically speaking, are we to continue our practice? We will look at practical actions that can be incorporated into our day-to-day living. For it is only through incorporation of the mundane that we can hope to sustain a spiritual endeavor.

# The Art of Joy

As we discussed in chapter 2, a central precept in the Jewish path is quite simple: Joy is the natural state of the soul. This precept is derived from two important principles of the Torah path. The first is that the quality of intimacy lies at the center of the universe; in other words, the world is not simply mechanistic and cold. It is built on relationship and personal connection. The second is that the world, in its deepest formulation, is always good. The cliché that everything happens for the best reflects this idea. Some things cannot be understood, but the basic nature of reality is sweet, filled with beauty and rejoicing. This is why, in the Torah, at the end of every day of creating the world, God concludes with the statement "And it was good" rather than "Well, this is pretty mediocre!"

One of the roads to joy is through *hitlahavut*, the path of ecstasy. *Hitlahavut* arises out of *chesed*, out of the well of loving-kindness. And it is to this path that we refer when we say that our task is to awaken the heart. This means that we are to reawaken ecstasy! When the soul unites with the Infinite, there is always ecstasy. King David, in Psalm 35, shouted, "All my bones shall say, Lord, who is like unto you!"[1] Even our bones realize that the process of God is constantly filling creation.

Ecstasy is the dance! Moment to moment, we are engaged in a joyful dance. But this is not a dance of drunkenness or loss of clarity. Ecstasy is not necessarily sloppy. Union with the One may be loud and boisterous, but it can also easily manifest in quiet, meditative joy. There is a story illustrating this: Once a young boy went to watch the great *tzaddik* Yitzhak of Vorki pray. He watched and watched, but the rebbe didn't move. He was absolutely still; not a muscle twitched. Disappointed, the boy returned home and complained to his father. *"Abba*, you said the rebbe was a holy saint. You said he was with God every moment. But I saw no sign of ecstasy."

His father replied, "A poor swimmer has to thrash about to stay afloat in the water. The good swimmer rests and lets the tide carry him."

Ecstasy is a flame, but it may be a quiet flame. The outward signs of ecstasy may be great, but in and of themselves they are no proof of enlightenment. The trick is to open the furnace doors of the heart. Each person reflects the spirit of the divine differently. I tend to become loud and boisterous. There is no single right way to reflect God's enlightenment any more than there is a single right way in which to love another person.

So how does one find joy and engage the heart? You have already begun. You both surrender to the power of God, which is a passive letting go, and actively reach out to the many joys and wonders that are given to us day to day. You elevate the soul by whatever means. You may take on the practice of daily meditation or blessings; you may decide to make a practice of treating the waitress who gives you your daily coffee with greater kindness. All of these practices serve to deepen your spirituality. As the soul is elevated, the heart will open. Conversely, as the heart opens, the soul is elevated.

And opening our hearts, we open more and more to the joyful compassion that is everywhere around us. *Chesed* is like the sea, and we are fish swimming in it. Much of our task (a happy one!) is to realize this—to open our mouths and drink. We can practice opening to *chesed* in every moment of our lives—when things are going well, and most especially when things are going poorly. We should practice it with the checkout person at the grocery store and the IRS official to whom we address our tax checks. We should try to be aware of it when anger arises toward our partner.

The art of setting up our own practice begins here. Find joy, engage the heart! And this means: Keep bringing your consciousness back to what you are doing.

# The Art of Community

Society today generates solitude. The ambitious may be rewarded with wealth, but often this ambition leads to increased solitude. There was once a man in need of help. He visited a therapist, but as he sat down the therapist said, "I am terribly busy. Please speak into this tape recorder and I'll listen to it later." About ten minutes later the therapist was horrified to find the client walking down the hallway, headed for the door. "What are you doing?" he cried. "Well, I'm terribly busy, too," said the man, "so I left my tape recorder, and it's talking to yours."

This absurd scenario reflects a very tragic reality. A therapist cannot help without *contact*. The entire root of help lies in the *personalness* of the contact. What we need is intimacy and connection. This need is fundamental and has not changed since creation. It is said that Abraham, the father of the Jewish people, used to sit in the doorway of his tent during the hottest part of the day, on the lookout for people traveling. If he saw someone, he would beckon them over and give them cool water, food, and perhaps a place to rest safely. This is the archetype of hospitality, and it captures an idea that the Jewish path reiterates in many places: that human life is quintessentially social and communal. Listen to how the psalm puts it: "How splendid and fine it is for beloved friends to be together!"[2]

Another story in our tradition describes Joseph, the son of Jacob. Joseph, you may remember, is taken off by his brothers and almost killed. Sold into slavery in Egypt, by a twist of fate (or the hand of God, depending on one's perspective), he rises to become Pharoah's right-hand man. Years later his brothers come to Egypt in rags, begging for bread because a famine is smothering the Middle East. They do not recognize their brother, sitting on his high throne, dressed in silk and gold. But he reveals himself and insists that they bring their families and friends to Egypt. "I will feed you and look after you, don't worry," he says. And he bursts into tears. A moment later his brothers do also.

There are many teachings that can be drawn from this story, but for me one shines out. Joseph had everything. He was wealthy beyond his dreams. He could have had women, despotic power, and more, if he chose. But none of this was his wish. He was a man who had everything but found that unless he had family he had nothing. Without community, he was poor beyond measure.

If we truly wish to make progress in our spiritual life, we must attach ourselves to community—even if we don't always like it! The power of the group, of the minyan, has the power to pull us forward. This is not to say that we should settle for just any community, but it is necessary to give ourselves over to a community during the time we are there. One cannot be halfhearted. One does not fall in love with someone only if they meet certain conditions! It is not the conditions that permit love; it is the internal decision to let go.

So, one important step in setting up your practice is to find a few kindred spirits and set up a meditation *chavurah*, study group. Get together for song and Shabbat. Meditate together. Discuss your learning and pool your resources to bring in a teacher periodically. Most of all, be patient with the process. If the first community doesn't gel, try again. Don't be discouraged. All beginnings are difficult. Perseverance will bring what you seek.

# Finding a Time and Place for Practice

The Ari, a fifteenth-century kabbalist, taught that the essence of each day's prayers is different. We know this from our own lives. Each day we need and desire different things. Our sages say, "If one's prayers are fixed, this is not a supplication," meaning that fluidity is an essential component of the spiritual life. This fluidity should be reflected in our meditation practice. For the purpose of daily practice is simply to make it easier to *become* that which we are practicing. Be steady—this is the key. Keep at it.

Regularity is helpful as you begin to meditate, as this provides a structure within which to be fluid. So it is important to find a place where you feel comfortable practicing your devotions—a "room of one's own," so to speak, although of course it can be just a corner of a room. It is also helpful if you can set aside a certain time, however brief, when you will meditate. Begin with ten minutes or so. Over the period of a few weeks, try to expand the time to twenty or thirty minutes. Some people prefer to meditate in the morning when they are fresh, others in the evening when the responsibilities of the day are finished. Either way is fine, but try to be consistent. These actions will yield tremendous fruit.

The busyness of each day steadily pulls us away from expanded consciousness. Be steadfast in your decisions about when and where you will meditate; this strengthens the intention (*kavannah*) and discipline of your *avodah*. But if you fall away from your practice, do not let guilt take hold of you. Examine the reasons why you stopped meditating. Perhaps you need to find a different place or set a different time. Learn what you can from getting sidetracked, and then simply start again.

# Finding Balance

When you begin to work within any spiritual tradition you may initially experience rapid swings in emotion. Often when you go from your day-to-day activities to a high sphere of grace and then back again, you can become angry or depressed. Your senses are slightly confused because of the sudden shift in insight, and when you come back to the mundane, all you want to do is return to that place of enlightenment. This is a very normal response and should not dissuade you from your *avodah*. Persist in your practice, and these shifts of consciousness will eventually diminish and disappear.

You may also notice that great clarities and great confusions will arise. There are aspects of the tradition that will seem to make tremendous sense and other parts that will seem completely absurd. There are types of practice that will work for you and others that will seem a waste of time. For example, sitting meditation may seem perfect for you, but the practice of making blessings seems silly and naive. Treating others with affectionate compassion may be immediately helpful, but lighting candles for Shabbat or saying a prayer feels inauthentic and contrived. This dance of the mind is normal. Stay with your overall practice and do not let yourself be sidetracked. That is, if you set yourself to light Shabbat candles, keep at it, but not to the point of becoming obsessed with it. If you do get sidetracked, take a deep breath and resume your practice.

Keep in mind that clarity and confusion are both self-perpetuating. These qualities of mind are reflected in our most mundane, everyday way of thinking. In everyday consciousness, the more often we repeat a certain way of perceiving, the easier it becomes to think in that groove. In the same way, the more we are able to open to joy and compassion in our spiritual practice, the easier *chesed* becomes. The more we dance, the better dancers we become. But confusions always abound. The first rule is, don't let yourself get lost in the details of your practice. This is especially important if you are practicing traditional Jewish rituals, where the details are potentially so daunting. Focus on the basic principles.

I have heard this story: Once there was a clever English philosopher who heard of an Indian fakir who was going around helping people experience God. But the Indian wasn't very sophisticated. Apparently he was illiterate. The Englishman sniffed when he heard this and decided to show him up. He traveled to where the fellow was staying and inquired sarcastically, "Tell me, O great fakir, what does the world rest upon?"

The Indian thought about this a while. "The world," he replied, "rests on the back of a giant water buffalo."

"Aha!" cried the philosopher, thinking he had him. "And what does the water buffalo rest on?"

"On the back of a giant horse."

"And what does the horse rest on?" he continued.

"On the back of a giant turtle."

Convinced this was the end, the Englishman pressed ahead. "And what does the turtle rest on?" he shouted in triumph.

"Oh, Sahib," the wise old man replied with a smile, "from there on, it is just turtles all the way down."

It is easy to outsmart ourselves. By getting lost in details, by mistaking intellectual sophistication for wisdom, we draw further away from union with the Infinite One. We cannot worry overmuch about what is the essence of God—it's just turtles all the way down. Many of the deepest questions cannot be answered with the rational mind. As a twelfth-century teacher said, "The inner, subtle essences can be contemplated only by sucking, not by knowing."[3] The infant receives nourishment not by thinking about the breast, but by sucking it. For some of the most profound questions of the soul, the simplest approach is the best. Too much intellectualism often prevents the experience of the thing itself.

A spiritual life is meant to move us more easily through the obstacles of life, but this is possible only when it leads us to a deeper knowledge of self. Sometimes the very disciplines that are meant to set us free catch us and hold us fast. Sometimes, for instance, the study of sacred texts becomes so all encompassing that we lose sight of the reality the texts are trying to put us in touch with. To make progress, we need balance, keeping our focus on the *Ayn Sof*, the Infinite One, and the experience of joy found in that One.

# Making a Place for the Infinite

Sometimes we view life very simply. A thing is good or bad, we like it or we don't. We view everything in the light of a few basic circumstances. For example, we may be happy about our children or thankful for our health, or we may dislike our job or experience misunderstanding with a loved one. At other times we view life more complexly. We know in an instant of insight that every single thing is supported by something under it. A vast network of interrelation is at work here—a web far too complex to be grasped with the mind alone.

Spiritually, the force we call God, the Infinite One, the Without-End, exists on both the simple and the complex levels. For even these two levels are contained within the whole of the Infinite One. In fact, there is no end to the nature of God. Once we enter into the realm of insight and bliss, remember, it's just turtles all the way down.

Entering this realm requires that we empty ourselves into the Infinite. For God cannot fill what is already full. So we empty ourselves of our ego, surrendering to the joyful purposes of the Infinite One; only then can God inhabit and perfume our whole being. Then we become partners in the complete joy the universe longs for. This is a very heady vision. But it reflects the intimate view of God that Jewish meditation and spirituality espouse.

But achieving this partnership requires a very real discipline. It requires that we give ourselves over on a daily basis, over and over, in all circumstances. There is a story that describes this discipline and commitment: On the day of rejoicing in the Torah (Simchat Torah), the disciples of the Roptchitzer rebbe were dancing ecstatically. Suddenly the rebbe raised his arms, and his face contorted with pain and grief. A hush fell over the madly dancing Chasidim. A moment later he cried out, "Does the army stop the struggle when a general dies? Keep dancing!" And so they did. Later they learned that the Karmarner rebbe, a great *tzaddik* and friend of their teacher, had died at that moment many hundreds of miles away.

We must not stop the dance.

But can we let ourselves dance? Can we bring ourselves *back to the dance?* Everything comes back to our power of choice. Everything depends on us—on the how and why of what we do. Constantly we are given opportunities to reevaluate ourselves and reintegrate what we have learned.

God constantly shows us the path, but She rarely repeats Herself.

There was once a cocky young fellow who decided to go to the master and embarrass him in front of the community. He hid a small bird in the palm of his hand and asked the master whether the bird was alive or dead. If the master said it was dead, he would open his hand and the bird would fly away. If he said it was alive, he could easily crush it in an instant in his grip. Either way the master would be shown to be not so wise or all seeing.

So he stood before the master and demanded, "Is the bird alive or dead?"

The master looked at him a moment and replied softly, "Really, my son, it all depends on you."

Where we are in our practice is dependent solely on us. It is all internal. The Sfat Emet (a Chasidic teacher of the early 1800s) taught that if one's love is dependent on cause (that is, some physical object), then with the passing of that cause, the love, too, will pass away.[4] But love that is not dependent on cause will remain. Soul love, the love that fills us after we have emptied ourselves of ego, is not dependent on cause; it is part of the Infinite itself. We are like a glass filled with seawater and sunk to the bottom of the sea. God, like the sea, fills us and surrounds us, but to recognize this, to *feel* this, is the struggle we face in our spiritual practice. And all the disciplines of *mitzvot*—meditation, prayer, and so on—are merely tools to help us attain this recognition.

Where does the Infinite One dwell? There is a wonderful place in the Torah where God describes the kind of place He can dwell: "Let them make me a sanctuary and I shall dwell in their midst."[5] Reread the line. In a subtle way, this line describes how to live a spiritual life. Where can the flame of love reside? Only where a sanctuary has been built for it. How one builds such a sanctuary differs enormously from person to person and moment to moment. But when you set aside a time and place for your meditation practice, you are laying the foundation for that sanctuary, and when you meditate with passion and regularity and commitment, cultivating the qualities of mind we have discussed and dealing with the obstacles that arise, you will soon find that you are raising the roof!

The spiritual endeavor can be likened to clearing a garden choked with weeds—weeds of wrong thinking and wrong action that must be pruned before there is space for the true garden to flourish and bloom. Of course this process can be difficult and frustrating. Sometimes, for every step forward, we seem to take two steps backward. But eventually our way becomes clearer, the light more abundant. Perhaps my own story will help to make this clear.

# My Experiences

While I was in India, I became used to a very simple existence filled with meditation, prayer, and various spiritual exercises. My teachers were itinerant sadhus (Hindu mendicants) who wandered through, and the Buddhist monks who lived in Sarnath, a nearby village. I woke to the cold bite of wind coming down from the Himalayas and the screams of peacocks, who in flight looked like a cross between beautiful dragons and hippopotamuses. My days were unencumbered by the need for work (American dollars in India went a long way), and the novelty of this different world and different civilization ensured that I did not grow bored.

Coming back to the States was a rude shock. I found the pace of American life overwhelming. I saw myself as quite the ascetic young guru. Most of my friends and family found me more than a little obnoxious. The *klippah* of pride was very strong in me!

In a very short time I began to feel that everything I had learned was slipping away. The wondrous insights I was used to receiving while meditating slowly dried up. Although I thought I was enlightened, I was becoming increasingly sour and short-tempered. The *klippot* of doubt and distraction reawoke in me with a vengeance.

Drastic efforts were needed, so I became a mendicant monk (though in a Jewish sort of way) here in the States. I gave away everything I owned, put on a robe, and began to wander around the country begging or doing odd jobs for a little food. I slept wherever I found myself. Either poverty was not so acute in those days as it is now, or it was more hidden; in any case, it was rare to see people living on the streets, especially where I wandered: shopping malls, middle-class housing developments. What I hoped to accomplish was to reawaken the sweetness and simplicity of my experience in India.

People were remarkably patient, but after about half a year of this, it became obvious to me that Americans were not used to young men in robes wandering the streets, nor were they likely to become so. While the majority of people were friendly enough, there were many who saw me only as a menace. Some threw stones, others were verbally abusive, one pulled a gun. For quite a while I translated all of this into my own high estimation of myself; in other words, people's lack of respect and adoration was simply a reflection of their own pathetically low spiritual attainment and, by contrast, of my own exquisite enlightenment. So I was back to where I started from—pride, distraction, all the *klippot*. So what had I learned? There were two profound differences from before and after my trip to India. One, I knew I could experience godliness for sustained amounts of time, and two, this perception could be lost. Insight, like a pearl of great worth, could be lost. I became more determined to learn and not lose what I acquired.

Near the end of this period, I found myself in southern California near a Catholic abbey— Benedictine, as I recall. I asked to be allowed to enter in order to regain some peace of mind. After six months on the streets, my thoughts were whirling in a frenzy of contradictory messages.

Of course this was a very peculiar move, since during this time I was still practicing a fairly strict Judaism. But all of this took place during the early seventies, and the abbot didn't seem to think there was anything strange about my request. He let me enter and said I could stay as long as I wished.

So I rose with the brothers at four or so in the morning and murmured my *Birkat Hashachar*, Jewish morning prayers, as they sang the morning office. It was an odd combination of energies, but our hearts were innocent, and for me at least, only good came of it. The light was increasing as I gave myself over to the life of the community. Each person there was a complete world, as the Tanya says—each soul beautiful and unique. People outside of the yeshiva or the monastery sometimes think that others enter such places to get away from the world. But it is not really a getting away. For the truest problems of the world—interpersonal understanding, patience, love, kindness, forgiveness—are brought into sharp focus in such a confined space. Your comrades cannot be avoided. You cannot run away from the conflicts that inevitably come up. One often enters that world in order to reorder priorities and grapple like Jacob with cosmic problems, only to find that these problems often boil down to the simplest scenarios of the soul. Truly, a yeshiva or monastery brings one face to face with what is needed in one's *avodah*.

For most of us, though, our future is not to be found in the yeshiva or the monastery. Most of us live within the strictures of work, mortgage, relationship, and so on. And in such a world, as we construct a spiritual *avodah*, difficulties arise in a thousand different shades and shapes.

Some of these obstacles are humorous, like my puzzlement on the problem, "If I am so enlightened, why am I so confused?" And some of our problems are deep, shaped by tragedy, and not lightly dismissed.

But my experiences in India, during my wandering, and in the monastery all kept pointing back to a central need. This was the need for an *avodah* that could be sustained, an *avodah* that would bring me closer to *the Ayn Sof* I hungered for.

*Avodah* never ceases. We come to the ceiling of our own spirituality and find over our heads another floor, which leads ever upward. In this sense life, and our spiritual practice, is always dynamic. There is no final there there. It goes ever on. This I have found in myself. Every new insight leads to a broadening of the horizon and deepening of soul.

# Building Community

Community building is potentially one of the deepest and most fulfilling practices we can do. Whether by our act of joining an already existing community or working to create a whole new community, allowing ourselves to become part of a greater whole brings us to a whole new level of insight.

As an exercise, community building can start out very modestly. It is common, after we have done a successful retreat or experienced a sudden deepening of our spiritual practice, to want to tell the world about it. So the first step is to talk about your spiritual insight—but in a modest way. Don't burden people with more information than they want to have. Listen with attention to their replies. Be skillful in letting each person have their say.

If you are sensitive and thoughtful with how you share the insights you are gaining from your *avodah*, people will probably begin seeking you out more and more in terms of hearing about it and engaging in conversation about it. At this juncture you might consider actually forming a study or a meditation group where you can practice and learn together.

As the group grows, remember, each communication counts. It is less important what you *know* than what you *are*. Our words may or may not resonate, but our *presence* in a loving, thoughtful way always serves as an example.

The exercise of building community comes back to our personal practice. The more present we are in joy and *chesed*, the easier it will be for us to increase the spiritual community around us.

Never be afraid of sharing the Torah path you have learned. It is powerful, and it will help others. At the same time, the heart of community building as a spiritual practice is similar to all the other avenues of practice. The point of it is to transform *you*. By your being transformed, you have a much better chance of helping in the transformation of your neighbor.

# Some Thoughts on the Nature of Enlightenment

*But the word is very close to you—*

*it is in your mouth and in your*

*heart, that you may do it.*

Deuteronomy 30:14

M uch of this book has tried to point out that every
moment in our lives is a spiritual moment; every deed
we do is potentially part of our spiritual practice. But no book
of this nature would be complete without some exploration of
the nature of enlightenment itself. Normally we think of
enlightenment *(mochin gadlut)* as a state of being that is free,
borderless, and full of bliss. But the notion of enlightenment
itself is a slippery one, and while it is impossible to write a
book on Jewish meditation and spirituality without touching
on it, it is equally important to frame it with a few
reservations—borders, if you like.

# The Dynamics of Enlightenment

E ach time we have an insight of any sort regarding our
own personality and how the world works, we burst
through a layer of consciousness to the next vista—what the
poet Francis Thompson (1859–1907) called "the long
savannas of the blue." Nor is there ever an end to the new
vistas that are possible. Even Moses, who attained the forty-
ninth level of enlightenment and died as he ascended to the
fiftieth, saw spreading out before him the next fifty levels of
wisdom.

Sometimes we think enlightenment has an ultimate
plateau. When we reach some final point of wisdom, we will
have embraced the ultimate grace and reached a final
enlightenment. But such a view of the universe is static, while
its process is actually dynamic. This dynamism can be
described in several ways, but an image used consistently
within the Jewish tradition is the metaphor of dance. The
Jewish path says only that we must embrace the dance. Open

to the music! As long as we are in the universe of *Assiyah*, the universe of physicality, our infinite soul contained in the tiny but beautiful vessel of the body, every aspect of our being is fluid. The great master Rebbe Nachman of Bratslav used to teach that "through music you can come to the level of prophecy. For the essence of *devekut* with God is through melody."[1] One of my great teachers, Joe Miller, used to say that "if you've listened to a word I've said, you're a damned fool. But if you are hearing what's in my heart, you're cooking on the BIG BURNER! To Feel Is for Real!" And then he would inevitably burst into song and do a jig.

# Confronting Our Borders

Each of us places borders around the vision of the Infinite. For borders help us to say what a thing is by their ability to also say what it is not. For example, every day in a traditionalist's life, a prayer is recited. This is the *Sh'ma Yisroel Adonai Elohenu Adonai Echad*: "Hear, O Israel, the Lord Our God the Lord Is One." The *Sh'ma* seeks to help trigger a deep awareness that all of the world is interwoven and without division, in spite of what our senses tell us. That is, the God (the totality of things) is One. Indeed, the *Sh'ma* is a meditation that insists ultimately that separation is illusion.

Yet even illusion has reality, and recognizing this forces us to recognize that our visions always contain borders. That is, as members of society we do live according to divisions we have created. We act based on choices concerning right and wrong, good and bad. But the Jewish tradition insists we should not accept these divisions as the deepest reality; they are, rather, a *disguised* reality. These guises are the *klippot*, the shells masking the inner reality of endless light.

And because our borders are ultimately *klippot*, they need to be tested regularly. The Nikolsburger rebbe would often use the sacrifice of Isaac as a teaching tool. "Look here," he would say. "God spoke to Abraham and commanded him to sacrifice the boy. So what's the big deal that he went and tried to do it?" The assumption being that if the Force of the Universe speaks to you and commands you, how can you possibly refuse?

Then the Nikolsburger rebbe would pause theatrically and answer, "All the previous enlightenment Abraham had achieved meant nothing at that moment, for every person constantly is confronted with their own limits. It does not matter whether we are on a high rung or a low one. Our test will be directed at exactly the place we are. This was the test for Abraham. All of his past holy deeds helped him not at all. Stripped of everything, each serious test forces us to confront the Force that makes the tests in the first place."

This is the nature of *avodah*, of constant practice.

We may become discouraged by our limits from time to time. My father used to tell me a story that may be helpful here. There was once a minister of state whom the king ordered to be executed. The minister threw himself at the king's feet and told him of a wonderful wooden horse he had that with the proper preparation could be made to fly.

"Bring me this magic horse," thundered the king, "and have him fly!"

"Oh, I cannot, Your Majesty," replied the minister, who explained that he needed a quiet place to make this miracle occur. "Lock me in a tower for safekeeping, if you wish, Your Majesty," he said, "but for peace of mind I need the food and companionship I am used to."

"And how long before the horse flies?" asked the king.

"About seven years, Your Majesty."

And so the king ordered it done. The minister's friends came to visit him in the beautiful and sumptuous tower that was his new home. "What are you doing?" they asked incredulously. "There is no way you can succeed at your work."

He replied, "Within seven years the king may die; there may be a revolution. And who knows— I might make that damned horse fly!"

Indeed, we may be able to make the damned horse fly! This is the vision of the Infinite, without borders. There is no end to what is possible, given a passionate and God-intoxicated heart. And to let this awakening to the Infinite happen to us—this is certainly within our power.

Each soul, reflected in the personality, has its bright gifts as well as its limitations. Our goal is to integrate both our strengths and weaknesses into our practice, to direct them toward enlightenment. Each of our borders, each of our *klippot*, must be woven with every other piece of the self. This weaving together of body, mind, and heart is part of the task of our *avodah*. No part of our soul can be cut off or discarded, no part of the deep structure that makes us *us* can be torn away. Each part must be *coaxed* into the weave of the whole. It must be *caressed* toward a greater and more proper use of its talents. It must be seduced. Then the borders we have placed around enlightenment will naturally expand, leading us further and further toward the Infinite.

We can so easily get caught up in our distinctions, in the borders we draw around the Infinite One. There is a Yiddish expression: A *grosser bord makht nit a Yid*, a big beard doesn't make a Jew. Modern life tends to see a split between everyday life and the eternal. Religion stands against this splitting. For it is also possible to see the great harmony, the great interweaving. Spirituality and life are one. Our *whole life* is the dance! The Rebbe Shlomo Carlebach often shouted at his Chasidim in the room, "Drunken! You must be drunk! It's in your heart! I need Chasidim who are drunk with love!" Drunk with love, we open our hearts, and love spills across the borders, across the splits between self and other, everyday and sacred.

Just as the Infinite is borderless, there is no limit to the amount of love we can give and receive. The Torah path commands us to love. It is the second statement of the *Sh'ma*: "And you shall love God with all your heart and might and strength…." But this is a strange command, really. How can we be commanded to love? We can be asked, cajoled—but ordered? Yet it is considered the fundamental principle of Torah. "You shall love your neighbor as yourself." But what if your neighbor is a fiend, a horror? We can answer this only with the admonition to look deeper. Every soul is a fragment of the Infinite. Each soul is a candle flame lit from the great sun of the Infinite One. And as it has been said, should we not love and feel compassion for such a pure thing that has become lost amid the shells of illusion?

Love your neighbor as yourself. This is a command to test the borders. It is a very active command. It seeks to reaffirm the fundamental connection among all aspects of creation. But this is not to say, Be passive in the face of oppression! The Jewish path is neither passive nor pacifist. One must respond to oppression and cruelty. We live in the universe of *Assiyah*, the realm of making, and we are called upon to be cocreators with God in this creation. Creation may require destruction—that is, proper and forceful action. A story illustrates this: Once a young woman came to her teacher and told him that every morning, as the group went into prayers, a young yeshiva student would get behind her and grope her. She was uncertain how best to deal with this. The master stroked his beard for a moment. "My friend," he said, "you should fill your heart with love, then turn around and deck him!"

# Beyond the Borders

The Jewish tradition has defined enlightenment in many different ways. There are aspects of the tradition that understand it supernaturally, as outside everyday consciousness, and other aspects that describe it purely psychologically, as an inner process. These definitions are not always kept separate; the psychological is often seen as an attribute of the supernatural and vice versa.

The Baal Shem Tov used to teach that where our mind is, that's where we are. This is a statement he repeated many times. His meaning was straightforward. We create a heaven or a hell every moment. But this creation arises from our own perception.

When the sage Hanina ben Tradyon was being martyred, his disciples gathered around him and pestered him. "What do you see, master?" they cried.

Hanina ben Tradyon had been wrapped in scrolls of Torah and was being burned. He called out, "The parchment burns, but the letters fly up to heaven!"

We know that during the Holocaust, many Chasidim sang and danced on the way to the gas chambers. Where did this spirit come from? What was their motivation? I do not mean to advocate senseless frivolity in the face of pain or anguish. But these stories point out that the world has many layers. Where we place our consciousness is the key to where we ourselves *are*.

To put it differently: The Baal Shem Tov, in teaching that we are where our minds are, was saying that in one moment we can be totally enlightened. And in the next moment we can fall away from it. Life's distractions are many, but the rewards are great. One may fall away from enlightenment in an instant, but it takes only another instant to regain it.

There is a story: Once there was a fish who started wondering, where was the ocean? She had heard all her life about the ocean and how we are born and die in it—how it surrounds us and how, when we surrender to it, we gain enlightenment. All this sounded very exciting to her, and she was determined to find it. So she swam from sea to sea, asking everyone she met whether they knew where to find the ocean. As far as I know, she is swimming still.

Finally, all that is required of us is to open ourselves to the ocean around us—to taste it and know that it is good. All viewpoints within the Jewish tradition agree to this. Enlightenment *is*; all we have to do is open up to it and let it fill us.

It has been described in our tradition that God is the infinite light and our soul is like a prism. Hold a prism up to the sun, and it will fill with innumerable permutations of light. Each prism moves light in different ways. In the same way, each person catches the Infinite differently. And this difference, from person to person, is very important to keep in mind.

I believe the Torah calls us to reunite with the Infinite Mother, the *Ayn Sof.* By opening ourselves to God, we are linking our drop of divinity with the Infinite One. The Jewish path advocates a life—and ultimately an enlightenment—in which a person lives fully in the world, savoring it, loving it, engaging *passionately* with it. Our task is not to remove our attachments to the world but to strengthen them—strengthen them in a true way, not simply in a way that increases the power of the ego. Each obstacle and each joy are equally gifts of the Infinite. For we have it within our grasp, through our own effort, to elevate our souls and open them to the great and sweeping melody of God.

# NOTES

## Chapter 1: Getting Our Bearings

1. The late Gershom Scholem (1897-1982) was the primary pioneer
   in reawakening the study of Jewish mysticism within the
   academic world. He is perhaps best known for his book *Major
   Trends in Jewish Mysticism* (New York: Schocken Books, 1954).
   Rivka Schatz-Uffenheimer is sometimes called his foremost
   student. Her body of work is not as large as Scholem's, but it is
   very valuable. In English her best work is *Hasidism as
   Mysticism: Quietistic Elements in Eighteenth-Century Hasidic
   Thought* (Princeton: Princeton Univ. Press, 1993). Moshe Idel
   and Daniel Matt can be thought of as the "new wave" in
   academic scholarship. Both of them have broken new ground in
   the unearthing and understanding of traditional mystical texts.
   Moshe Idel's output is large and growing. He is probably best
   known for his *Kabbalah: New Perspectives* (New Haven: Yale
   Univ. Press, 1988). Daniel Matt is perhaps the best Hebrew
   translator living today. He has several excellent books out,
   including a masterful translation of Zohar and a book titled *The
   Essential Kabbalah* (San Francisco: HarperSanFrancisco, 1995),
   a series of short translations from a wide variety of mystical and
   spiritual Jewish texts.

2. The late Aryeh Kaplan was prodigious in exposing Jewish
   meditation to a larger audience. He translated huge amounts of
   material and made accessible whole realms of discourse on the
   subject. It is not altogether clear exactly how much meditation he
   did himself. Rebbe Zalman Schachter-Shalomi is a modern Torah
   giant familiar with all areas of Jewish spirituality, including the
   ins and outs of meditation. Jonathan Omer-Man is an excellent
   teacher living in Los Angeles. He is the director of Metivta, a
   school teaching Jewish spirituality. David Cooper is another
   excellent teacher living in the wilds of Colorado, where he
   directs a retreat center. He is the author of several books

including *Renewing Your Soul* (San Francisco: HarperSanFrancisco, 1995).

3. Mic. 6:6–8.

4. Wherever possible, I have avoided using the masculine pronoun exclusively, choosing to alternate between masculine and feminine to indicate that the path is open to all. Historical records often focus on male students, but the meditation tradition has always included women as well.

5. Menashe Miller, *Ish ha-Pele* (Jerusalem: Machon Zecher Naftali, 1987), 69.

6. Keter Shem Tov, *Aaron of Apt* (Jerusalem, 1968), 42.

7. Yitzhak Buxbaum, quoting the Arizal, *Sefer Haredim*, chap. 65, in Jason Aaronson, *Jewish Spiritual Practices* (Northvale, NJ: Jason Aaronson, 1994), 379.

8. Quoted in *Liqutei Yeqarim: Teaching Baal Shem Tov and Maggid of Mezritch*, compiled by Tisacher Baer of Zlatchov (Lemberg, 1865), 18b–c.

9. Matt, *The Essential Kabbalah*, 71, trans. from Dov Baer, *Maggid Devarav I'Ya'aqov.*

10. Matt, *The Essential Kabbalah*, 150, trans. from Alexander Susskind (eighteenth century), *Yesod v'Shoresh ha-Avodah* (Jerusalem: 1968).


## Chapter 2: Learning Some Basic Concepts

1. Louis Jacobs, *Hasidic Prayer* (New York: Schocken Books, 1972), 83.

2. Moses De Leon, quoted in Gershom Scholem, *Major Trends in Jewish Mysticism* (New York: Schocken Books, 1954), 223.

3. Rebbe Levi Yitzhak, *Kedushat Levi* (Jerusalem, 1958).

4. Ps. 19:2–5.

5. Z'vat Haribash, quoted in Joseph Dan, *Teaching of the Hasidism* (West Orange, NJ: Library of Jewish Studies, Behrman House, 1983), 139.

6. Deut. 29:11–14.

7. Adapted from Maor v'Shemesh, Nitzavim. Kalanamous Kalman (Brooklyn: Kriyat Seferi).

8. Rebbe Schneur Zalman, *Heyichud v'Haemunah* (n.p., n.d.).

## Chapter 3: Understanding the Four Qualities of Consciousness

1. Midrash, *Vayikra Rabbah* 5:8.

2. Quoted in Aaron Greenberg, *Iturei Torah* (Tel Aviv: Yavneh Publishing, 1989), 161.

3. Moses Maimonides, *Hilchot T'murah* 4:13.

4. Megilat Koheleth. (Spring Valley, NY: Feldheim, 1994), 94–95.

5. Quoted in Philip Novak, ed., *The World's Wisdom* (San Francisco: HarperSanFrancisco, 1995), 43.

6. *Sefer Haredim*, chap. 9, no. 10.

7. The Keter Shem Tov, *Shem*, chap. 3.

8. Likkutim Yekarim, 9b.

9. Conversation with Shlomo Carlebach z'l.

## Chapter 4: Recognizing Obstacles

1. Midrash Pinchas, no. 21, Rabbi Pinchas Shapiro of Koretz.

2. As told to Rebbe YaakovYosef of Polonye (1704–1794), VaYakehl (author's translation).

3. Quoted in *Sefer Baal Shem Tov*, Bereshit (Jerusalem, 1962).

4. Morris Faierstein, *All Is in the Hands of Heaven: The Teachings of Rabbi Mordecai Joseph Leine* (New York: Yeshiva Univ. Press, 1989), 32.

## Chapter 5: Setting Up Your Own Practice

1. Ps. 35:10.

2. Ps. 133:1–2.

3. Daniel Matt, *The Essential Kabbalah* (San Francisco: HarperSanFrancisco, 1995), 113, quoting Isaac the Blind (twelfth century), commentary on *Sefer Yetsirah.*

4. Adapted from Yehuda Aryeh Hein, ed., *Shir Hashirim Im Perush Sefat Emet* (Jerusalem, 1955), 6.

5. Exod. 25:8.

## Epilogue: Some Thoughts on the Nature of Enlightenment

1. Nachman of Bratslav, *Likkutei Atzot*, compiled by Reb Noson, translated by Avraham Greenbaum (Jerusalem: Breslov Research Institute, 1983).

# GLOSSARY

*ahavah.* Love.

*avodah.* Work; spiritual practice.

*ayin.* Place of nothingness.

*Ayn Sof.* The Without-End.

*bitul hayesh.* Annihilation of that which is; the Infinite.

*chesed.* Joyful compassion.

*cheshbon nefesh.* A soul accounting.

*chavurah.* Study group.

*chevrah.* Community.

*chokhmat lev.* Wisdom of the heart.

*devekut.* Rapturous attachment; one of the four states of mind cultivated in Jewish meditation practice.

*Echad; echad.* The One, God; unity, oneness.

*eseret hadibrot.* The Ten Commandments.

*gashmiyut.* The play of illusion and physicality.

*gevurah.* Strictness, harshness, control, strength.

*gilgulim.* Reincarnations.

*hitbodedut.* A style of meditation that is inner directed.

*hitbonenut.* A style of meditation that is externally focused.

*hitlahavut.* The path of ecstasy, the way of heart.

*kavannah.* Passionate intentionality; one of the four states of mind cultivated in Jewish meditation practice.

*klippah (pl.: klippot).* Obstacle; literally, shell or husk.

*korban.* Sacrifice.

*malach hamavet.* The angel of death.

*mitzvah (pl.: mitzvot).* Action, specific practice.

*mochin gadlut.* Great Mind; enlightenment.

*m'sirah.* Surrender; one of the four states of mind cultivated in Jewish meditation practice.

*nava.* To gush, to flow forth.

*navach.* To cry out.

*navuv.* To be hollow.

*navi.* Prophet.

*pardes.* Garden.

*rachamim.* Mercy.

*ratzon.* Will; one of the four states of mind cultivated in Jewish meditation practice.

*shefa.* Flow.

*Shoah.* Holocaust.

*t'fillin (sing.: t'fillah).* Small leather boxes filled with prayers and blessings that are worn on the upper arm and forehead during morning prayers.

*tikkun.* Healing.

*tikkun olam.* The repairing or healing of the world.

*tzaddik.* A fully enlightened being.

# ABOUT JEWISH LIGHTS

People of all faiths and backgrounds yearn for books that attract, engage, educate, and spiritually inspire.

Our principal goal is to stimulate thought and help all people learn about who the Jewish People are, where they come from, and what the future can be made to hold. While people of our diverse Jewish heritage are the primary audience, our books speak to people in the Christian world as well and will broaden their understanding of Judaism and the roots of their own faith.

We bring to you authors who are at the forefront of spiritual thought and experience. While each has something different to say, they all say it in a voice that you can hear.

Our books are designed to welcome you and then to engage, stimulate, and inspire. We judge our success not only by whether or not our books are beautiful and commercially successful, but by whether or not they make a difference in your life.

For your information and convenience, at the back of this book we have provided a list of other Jewish Lights books you might find interesting and useful. They cover all the categories of your life:

Bar / Bat Mitzvah • Bible Study / Midrash • Children's Books • Congregation Resources • Current Events / History • Ecology / Environment • Fiction: Mystery, Science Fiction • Grief / Healing • Holidays / Holy Days • Inspiration • Kabbalah / Mysticism / Enneagram • Life Cycle • Meditation • Men's Interest • Parenting • Prayer / Ritual / Sacred Practice • Social Justice • Spirituality • Theology / Philosophy • Travel • Twelve Steps • Women's Interest

**Stuart M. Matlins, Publisher**

Jewish Lights books are available from better bookstores.
Try your bookstore first.

www.jewishlights.com

For more information about each book,
visit our website at www.jewishlights.com

**Avram Davis** earned his Ph.D. at the University of California, Santa Cruz. He is the founder and co-director of Chochmat HaLev, a center dedicated to Jewish spirituality and meditation. He is the co-author of *Judaic Mysticism* (Hyperion) and editor of *Meditation from the Heart of Judaism: Today's Teachers Share Their Practices, Techniques, and Faith* (Jewish Lights).

"A wonderful book written like a prayer by a true disciple who sees all paths to the spirit as his own."
    —CARL A. HAMMERSCHLAG, M.D., psychiatrist, teacher, healer, author of *The Dancing Healers* and *The Theft of the Spirit*

**For People of All Faiths, All Backgrounds**
JEWISH LIGHTS PUBLISHING

**www.jewishlights.com**

Cover design: Bridgett Taylor

9 781683 364504